The Press

A Critical Look From the Inside

Edited by A. Kent MacDougall

DOW JONES BOOKS
PRINCETON, NEW JERSEY

Introduction

Editors and publishers can dish it out, but until recently they rarely had to take it. True, a handful of professional press critics have decried the sad state of the Fourth Estate for decades, but their indictments usually have been confined to scholarly journals and erudite books with limited readership and little impact. Criticism of the press in the press itself has been as scarce as editorials knocking low second-class postage rates. Newspapers regularly spike unfavorable news about themselves and even about competitors, fearing turnabout would be foul play.

But like the flag and motherhood and even Sunday school, the press is no longer immune from attack. High government officials, irked that some newspapers sometimes fail to parrot the party line, have taken the "liberal" press to task—and occasionally to court. Television, often the butt of jibes in the press, has retaliated with programs, such as "Behind the Lines" in New York, that turn a critical camera on press performance. Newsmen in a dozen cities have started journalism reviews. Their stock in trade is exposing newspaper publishers who tailor the product less to serve readers than to please advertisers, powerful politicians and fellow businessmen.

Several years before the first of these local journalism reviews appeared, The Wall Street Journal significantly stepped up its coverage of the press. It took to running in-depth profiles of colorful, controversial publications, as well as spotlighting such significant trends as growing concentration of news media ownership. So extensive did The Wall Street Journal's coverage become that some journalists dubbed it The Wall Street Journalism Review.

Introduction

The twenty articles in this book are the best of
the sixty major features on the press that The Wall
Street Journal has published since 1966. Here are the
stories of some of the giants and pygmies of American
journalism, their successes and failures, their high-
and low-minded policies and practices. The nation's
largest-circulation newspaper, the New York News, is
profiled here, along with the world's best-selling magazine, the Reader's Digest. Variety, the small spunky
Bible of Broadway, gets a generally favorable review.
More mixed is the report on the Associated Press and
United Press International, which together disseminate
most of the national and international news that
Americans read and listen to. Clive Barnes, perhaps
the fastest typewriter in the East, is here, alongside
Art Buchwald, undoubtedly the funniest man in the
Capital.

Some editors and publishers have profited from
having their shortcomings reported in the Journal. The
Journal's article on the "New Journalism" prompted
one magazine, which is sometimes accused of masquer-
ading fiction as fact, to start warning readers when
novelistic devices are used in supposedly non-fiction
articles. On the other hand, some thin-skinned publishers have reacted with less than good grace. One
newspaper, angered by its profile in the Journal, can-
celled a $40,000 advertising campaign in the Journal.
(It has since returned to the fold.)

Taken together, these pieces do not paint a pretty
picture of the press. But they do afford a backstage
peek at the morals, mentality and motives of those
who write, edit and own the nation's newspapers and
magazines, and their often bizarre products and By-
zantine operations.

—A. KENT MACDOUGALL
Editor

Contents

Contents

New York Daily News

THE New York Daily News doesn't mince words.
Says an editorial tirade against the United Nations: "Aw, the hell with this sweetness and light. We still say that glass cigar box is jammed with pompous do-gooders, nervy deadbeats, moochers, saboteurs, spies and traitors, and that we . . . (should) throw the bums out."

Says a headline over a story about Mandy Rice-Davies, a party girl in Britain's Profumo scandal who criticized actor Douglas Fairbanks Jr.: QUEEN OF TARTS CALLS DOUG A CRUMB.

Says the paper of Fidel Castro: "That bearded little Communist cockroach in Havana." Of Communists in general: "The only good Red is a dead Red." Of collegiate dissenters: "Kooks and kookettes, Reds, Pinks, punks and dupes." Of liberals: "Bleeding hearts."

This kind of forthright writing is sprinkled in and around stories and pictures on sex, scandal, pathos and human frailty. In addition, the tightly written paper has what is generally considered excellent coverage of crimes and disasters, a good sports section and 17 comic strips, including Dick Tracy.

This formula has made the seven-cent Daily News the most widely sold newspaper in America, with weekday circulation of 2.1 million. On Sundays, when the paper costs 20 cents, circulation is 3.1 million.

Yet, the News "isn't an important paper," says

Frank Holeman, a News editor in New York who formerly was on the paper's Washington staff. "If Rusk wants to launch a trial balloon he calls Scotty Reston" of the New York Times, he says. "If the cops knock off a cat house on 72nd Street, they call us." The News is seldom listed among the 10 best papers in the nation.

The paper's real problem though, is that fewer persons want to read about those 72nd Street raids than before. In the past 20 years, circulation of "New York's Picture Newspaper" has fallen by 300,000 on weekdays and by nearly 1.6 million on Sunday. And this despite the death a few years ago of the New York Mirror, which once matched its fellow tabloid scandal for scandal. News profit fell in 1966 from 1965.

(In the same 20 years, circulation of the Times, which now is the only general-interest competitor of the News in the morning, increased to 873,000 on weekdays from 556,000 and to 1.5 million on Sundays from 1.1 million. Its profit has been rising steadily.)

"Readers have become a little more sophisticated and perhaps we haven't kept abreast," says Jack E. Underwood, circulation manager of the News. "A whole new generation has grown up" since founder Joseph Medill Patterson died in 1946. Capt. Patterson—he was a captain in World War I and was called Captain from then on—founded the News in 1919 and ran the paper on the theory of "Tell it to Sweeney—the Stuyvesants will take care of themselves." But now, says Mr. Underwood, "The trouble is there are fewer Sweeneys around to tell it to."

So the News has decided to provide some filling for the Stuyvesants and the rest of the upper crust. Sort of. It definitely isn't giving up sex (recent major headlines include GALLEASE TRIAL EXPECTED TO HEAR LOVELORD TODAY and MAID BACK WITH BABY & RAPE TALE) or crime (MOD GIRL SLAIN NEAR

WALL ST.) But it has doubled its financial news to a full page daily and it is beefing up its science coverage, which just received a blow when chief science writer Richard Lyons was hired away by the Times.

It also plans to tone down its flamboyant makeup a bit, increasing the size of the body type and decreasing the size of some headlines.

The News also is running promotional ads to lure the more affluent reader. It claims that "almost a quarter of a million News readers come from families with incomes over $20,000" and it asks such questions as, "Are You Secure Enough to Read the News at the Waldorf? Your Boss Is" and "Can a Vassar Graduate Find Happiness With the News?" It boasts that such notables as producer David Merrick, opera singer Rise Stevens, former Esso Standard President Stanley C. Hope and ballerina Melissa Hayden all read the News religiously.

Nevertheless, "any changes we make are going to be step by step," says William A. Casselman, the executive editor. "We hope to avoid shocking readers."

Most News readers probably are shock proof. Court reporter Alfred Albelli almost daily turns up lurid divorce cases. Other News reporters, especially William Federici, have a close rapport with the police that often leads to shocking exclusives. News photographers cruise the city in 11 cars equipped with radios to receive police and office calls.

"The cops think the world of us because we have carried so many crusades for them," says Mr. Federici. "I'm sure we had an awful lot to do with defeating the civilian review board," a proposal by Mayor John Lindsay that would have had civilians dominating a board to investigate complaints, such as allegations of brutality, against the police.

When the city's voters defeated the board, the News

hailed the move editorially as freeing "the world's finest metropolitan police force from the threat of hobbles and handicaps inflicted by cop-haters, Meddlesome Matties, Nervous Nellies and Communists." The News rarely criticizes the force as a whole, though it occasionally castigates individuals.

In return for this friendship and, some sources say, for payments from the News, the police provide tips to the paper. The News denies that it pays police for tips, and Mr. Federici says his leads often come from "drinking buddy" relationships with many policemen. Mr. Federici also has some friendships on the other side of the law—"guys I grew up with who turned out no good" —and these led him to recover in 1965 the $140,000 Delong Ruby, which had been stolen from the American Museum of Natural History here.

But linking the News exclusively to crime and sensation is wrong, asserts executive editor Casselman. It's true that the careful reader can always find at least a paragraph on significant world events, but he usually must look elsewhere for analysis and interpretation.

"This cliche that we specialize in sex and sensation is in error," says the 63-year-old executive editor. In trade ads beamed at advertisers in the eight-column Times, the five-column News asks, "What makes you think morality only comes in eight columns?"

In fact, the News shuns stories of wayward priests, child molesters and homosexuals. "There's nothing sexy about an unnatural sex story," says Mr. Holeman, who is assistant to Mr. Casselman. Other perversions don't seem to bother it so much. When police raided the alleged headquarters of a nationwide sex-and-sadism operation in Newark, N.J., not so long ago, the News played it as the top story of the day, headlining it: RAID BLONDE'S TORTURE HOUSE. WHIPS, CHAINS

IN NEWARK MANSION. The Times put the story on
Page 21.

The News, headquartered in a modern building at
42nd Street and Second Avenue, has 600 newsmen, including 57 photographers and 2 pilots who fly photographers around, on its staff of 5,000. It has six full-time
correspondents abroad and nine staffers in Washington, where bureau chief Ted Lewis is widely respected
for his political savvy. (Mr. Lewis and James Desmond,
who covers New York State politics, also contribute to
the Nation, a weekly that stands for nearly everything
the News opposes.)

Despite the News' huge audience—the nation's second biggest daily, The Wall Street Journal, has about
half the weekday circulation of the News—few Washington bigwigs cater to it. It does get some scoops,
though. It was the first to say, for instance, that Bill D.
Moyers was quitting as Presidential press secretary.
However, a big scoop of 1966, that Lynda Bird Johnson
would marry actor George Hamilton before the year was
out, didn't prove as accurate.

The staff is heavy with phony bylines and with
old-timers. Society editor "Nancy Randolph" is really
Julia McCarthy, etiquette editor "Elinor Ames" is really
Addis Durning, and help-the-needy columnist "Sally
Joy Brown" is really Elizabeth LaRosa. "Kate Cameron," movie critic for 35 years until her retirement this
year, is Loretta King, the sister of the widow of Capt.
Patterson. (His widow, Mary King Patterson, is still active as women's editor, though in her 80s.) The phony
name system was started by Capt. Patterson, who didn't
want the readers to be disappointed when a critic or
writer retired or died; the names usually carry on,
though the name of "Kate Cameron" was retired with
Miss King.

There is no mandatory retirement age at the News.

Editor Richard W. Clarke is 70. Political writer Dick Lee is 80. Radio-TV editor Ben Gross, on the News since 1925, won't give his age. There are many others over 65. Some old staffers earn their keep, executives say. Others don't. "There are a lot of people stumbling around here who are old in years and thinking and who ought to be kicked the hell out," says a young executive. They are kept on largely because of the paternalistic policies of Capt. Patterson.

This job security — it's next to impossible to get fired at the News—partially compensates for the lower editorial salaries at the News than at the Times. But it doesn't always offset the money. Many editorial staffers supplement their salaries by moonlighting. Sports columnists Gene Ward and Dick Young are football commentators on radio. Night city editor Howard Wantuck and city hall reporter Dominick Peluso practice law. Several deskmen spend their days off working at other papers.

In addition, the News-men can pick up extra cash for an especially good story, headline, caption or picture. Among the memorable headlines was one on a story about a robbery at the News' Brooklyn printing plant. It said: WE WUZ ROBBED. On a story about an Italian prosecutor accusing Gina Lollobrigida of acting indecently in a film, the News wrote:

CHARGES GINA
WAS OBSCENA
ON LA SCREENA

The headline writers seem to have fun at their jobs. They appear to be awed by no man. They refer to Gov. Nelson Rockefeller as "Rock" or "Guv," to Vice President Hubert H. Humphrey as "Humph" and to Lewis S. Rosenstiel, chairman of Schenley Industries Inc., as "Whisky Big."

The News' picture coverage ranks as high as its

headlines in journalists' opinions. A Times executive says, "We run as many pictures as the Daily News but they're not as good." The News puts its best picture of the day on page one, regardless of whether it was taken by a staff photographer or supplied by a wire service. Though 10 News photographers attended Luci Johnson's wedding in Washington, the page one picture came from United Press International.

The News retouches 95% of the photos it uses, and sometimes its eight retouchers are too skillful. In August 1965 news services supplied photos of a young woman boarding Frank Sinatra's chartered yacht off Hyannis Port, Mass. The shots were taken from a distance and the woman's face was fuzzy. The news services misidentified her as Jacqueline Kennedy, and the News, along with many other newspapers, printed the error. But the woman in the News picture looked exactly like Mrs. Kennedy, thanks to the neat work of a retoucher.

One thing that hasn't been facelifted at the News in more than 25 years is the editorial policy. Capt. Patterson began as a socialist, became a New Deal Democrat, fell out with President Roosevelt over foreign policy in the late 1930s and ended up as an ultra-conservative and ultra-nationalist. His successors are of like conservative mind.

Reuben Maury, an energetic 67-year-old, has written most News editorials since 1926, changing his tune as the Captain changed his. For 10 years, Mr. Maury also contributed editorials to Collier's magazine, which often meant disagreeing with himself in print.

"An editorial writer is like a lawyer or a public relations man," he explains. "His job is to make the best possible case for the client." Mr. Maury, who writes in a breezy, belligerent style, says he shares 98% of the News' views and "doesn't care" about the other 2%.

The News is against a lot of things—especially communism and liberalism—but it also is for some things. It is, for instance, for "the poor old cigaret," which it says is under attack by "fright merchants" linking it to cancer and other ills. (Mr. Maury gave up smoking on doctor's orders.) It also is for unleashing Chiang Kai-shek to wipe out Red China's nuclear facilities with U.S. planes and bombs.

If the News leaves little doubt where it stands, its detractors are equally forthright. James Aronson, editor of the National Guardian, a left-wing weekly, calls the News "an obese, malevolent fish wife, screaming journalistic obscenities at more than two million persons a day, exhorting them to go out and kill a Commie for Christ—or even just for fun."

Nat Hentoff, a writer and critic, says the News "views things with stunning oversimplification, and, though edited for the workingman, doesn't fight for him." A News writer says, "The News could be the greatest paper as well as the biggest, but we are against things that are good for most people. We are the paper of the masses, but we sound like the board of directors."

Some observers say the News lets it editorial feelings slip into news stories, such as the story saying that three women pacifists who had visited North Vietnam "could be faulted for inaccuracy and naivete in their reports." But Kitty Hanson, who has won many awards for her penetrating series on such problems as Harlem street gangs and unwed mothers, says her conclusions often "fly violently in the face of editorial policy."

Many readers seem to like the blunt, conservative position of the paper. About 700 readers write letters to the editor each week, and some of these writers are more outspoken than is Mr. Maury. One letter used recently said, "If we are going to win (in Vietnam) let us not be polite about it. Let us antagonize, bombardize, smasherize and, if necessary, atomize the swine until they come crawling on their knees, with nothing in sight but unconditional surrender."

The News also gets about 1,200 letters a week from readers contributing a "bright saying" or "household hint" in hopes that it will be printed and they will get $5. Some 13,000 persons write in each week for dress patterns and needlework books, most of which cost money. And in a promotional contest last year, the News received 11.5 million entries.

This response spells rapport to editor Clarke. "One of the reasons for our success is the rather close association we maintain with our readers," he says.

To keep readers thinking about it, the News advertises heavily on radio, runs contests with cash prizes and sponsors a slew of special events. For high school students, there's an art show, science fair, chorus and orchestra concert, baseball clinic and track meet. The paper packs Madison Square Garden each fall for its amateur dance contest, the Harvest Moon Ball, and each spring for the New York Golden Gloves, an amateur boxing contest it sponsors.

The News also runs election polls, checking 30,000 registered voters in the state for three weeks before elections as a circulation-building feature. It has correctly called the winner in 23 of 26 elections since 1928, with one of the misses coming last November when it predicted Democrat Frank O'Connor would unseat Republican Gov. Rockefeller.

The promotions are almost all aimed at the ordinary workingman—and so is much of the paper. The movie, drama, art and music reviews are less than sophisticated. "The News' standards of movie entertainment are more in keeping with mass tastes than with the artistic and creative aspects that motivate other critics," says Jonas Rosenfield, a vice president of Twentieth Century-Fox Film Corp.

The offbeat movie Blow-Up, voted the best film of 1966 by the National Society of Film Critics, got only two stars on the News' fourstar rating system.

Though the News doesn't review books, it, almost alone among newspapers, serializes novels. It also runs short stories. Readership is relatively low, some staffers suspect, but no change is likely. "Capt. Patterson thought fiction was a great thing," says Mr. Clarke, the editor, explaining the stories are a holdover from the Patterson era. But he adds, "We don't want to tinker with a successful formula."

—A. KENT MacDOUGALL

1967

Washington Post

EARLY in 1970 the Washington Post gave extensive coverage to the case of a hippie girl charged with murdering her father. Critics said the Post blew the story out of proportion. One critic charged sarcastically that the story was played up in the Post because the girl and her friends "are hippies—and we all know what that means. A hippie is Charlie Manson: So a hippie is a murderer."

Criticism of newspapers is commonplace today, but this particular protest came from an unusual source. The attack on the Washington Post appeared in an editorial—in the Washington Post. "We had deplored this (sensationalism) for other papers, so we really couldn't remain silent about ourselves," explains Philip L. Geyelin, the editor of the Post's editorial pages.

That's what readers have come to expect of the Post in recent years. Nothing is sacred—least of all itself—on the capital's biggest and most influential paper. One columnist denounces another, in print, as an "old screech owl of war." A reporter breaks a story about a dispute between two Post columnists. Nearly everyone takes pot-shots at friends of the owner. And an outsider who denounces the Post as "the most irritating paper in the country" is subsequently hired for a top job on the publication.

The paper doesn't limit its attacks to self-flagellation. Its plain-spoken editorials lash out regularly at friend and foe—especially such foes as Richard Nixon and Spiro Agnew—and its news columns routinely uncover local, national and world wrongs. Its political columnists range from one extreme to the other, and its society writers are omnipresent—so none of the mighty or their consorts is immune from attack or ridicule.

All this brings the Washington Post fans and foes. The morning paper's circulation, 502,000 daily and 663,000 on Sunday, far surpasses that of the Evening Star, which has 305,000 daily and 358,000 on Sunday. The Post also dominates in both advertising and influence, two areas where the Star formerly was No. 1. Also, the Post, with estimated pretax profit of $10 million in 1969, considerably outearns the Star. A third Washington paper, the Daily News, an evening tabloid owned by the Scripps-Howard chain, ranks last in circulation, advertising, earnings and, especially, influence.

One regular Post reader is Vice President Spiro Agnew, and he often doesn't like what he reads. To him, the Post is part of that subversive Eastern liberal establishment that he dislikes so much, and he regularly attacks the paper in public and in private. (The feeling is mutual. The Post supported Mr. Agnew for governor of Maryland, but it compared his nomination for the Vice Presidency with the appointment by the Roman emperor Caligula of his horse as proconsul. An Agnew associate says the comment "was the lowest blow he has ever received in politics.")

Another foe is Sen. Barry Goldwater, who says he reads the Post "because it has a good comic section." (Its 28 strips, close to a record for a U.S. daily, run from Peanuts to Dick Tracy to Mary Worth.) President Eisenhower used to have the sports pages cut out and brought to him so he wouldn't have to read the rest of the paper. (Its sports pages are considered merely adequate and overly fawning by many sports fans.) And

Richard Nixon refused to subscribe when he was Vice President because he didn't want his daughters to see the Herblock cartoons of him looking sinister and stubbly faced. (Herblock gave Mr. Nixon a shave when he was elected, but the cartoons are still less than flattering.) Ronald Ziegler, White House press secretary, reflects the Administration's attitude toward the paper by even refusing to acknowledge directly that Mr. Nixon reads the Post now. He will say only that "the President reads those papers that are available in Washington."

One reason Administration officials don't care for the Post is that its persistent attacks on the Haynsworth and Carswell nominations to the Supreme Court are believed to have helped defeat those nominations. At one point, a Herblock cartoon depicted Judge G. Harrold Carswell emerging from a garbage can.

The Post has other than political critics. Some critics say that Post reporters are permitted to advocate causes in their news stories. Others say the paper's news judgment is sometimes atrocious—on one recent day the news of the settlement of the California grape strike and the British dock strike was on inside pages of the Post, while a piece on computerization of some local traffic lights appeared on page one.

Critics also contend the paper's foreign coverage is spotty it has no men assigned to Egypt or Israel, for instance—and that too often the Post has to scramble to catch up on a major domestic story where it neglected to assign a reporter. "They're a long way from our class," flatly states A. M. Rosenthal, managing editor of the New York Times.

Perhaps, but if there is a gap the Post is closing it every day. Though they are in different cities, the Washington Post and the New York Times are each other's main competitor, top editors of both papers say. Every night each paper gets a photo transmission of the other's front page and puts its reporters to work on any big story that the competitor has exclusively. (As a result, the Post sometimes keeps exclusives out of its first edition.) The Times' recent decision to add a second page for editorial columns was reportedly inspired by the Post's success with a similar format.

"In the 1950s, the Times had serious journalism in Washington all to itself," claims Max Frankel, the Times bureau chief here. "Now we feel their competition very keenly." The Times still sells far more papers in Washington (23,000 daily and 31,000 Sunday) than the Post sells in New York (1,300 daily and 1,000 Sunday) —but until recently virtually nobody in New York bothered to read the Post.

"We're never going to be best the way the New York Times is best because we have a different situation here," says Katharine Graham, president and majority stockholder of the Washington Post Co. and publisher of the paper. "They can write to a highly educated, specialized audience, but we are a mass paper." Indeed, as the only morning paper in the capital, the paper must cater to rich and poor, smart and not-so-smart, urbanite and suburbanite. Besides being hometown paper to 535 Congressmen, it also is hometown paper to about 110,000 ghetto dwellers. And it has a larger circulation in Virginia than any paper published in that state.

In trying to be all things to all men, the Post contains a lot of trivia mixed in with the news. It runs two columns on advice to the lovelorn, a question-and-answer column on pets and much other material that serious readers consider drivel. (Example: "Question: My 14-year-old grandson scrambles four large eggs three or four times a week for breakfast. Is this too many eggs for a 14-year-old boy to eat at one time? Answer: Healthy 14-year-olds have a lot of sudden growing to do.

Four large eggs for breakfast is a harmless way to start his busy day.")

Still, some people think Mrs. Graham tends to be too modest. There are some who think the Post is the very best paper in the nation in its editorials and investigative reporting, and, overall, second only to the New York Times. If that is so, Mrs. Graham deserves most of the credit. The Washington Post was purchased in 1933 by her father, Eugene Meyer, an immigrant's son who had made a fortune in investment banking. For 15 years, he ran it as a second-rate, largely red ink operation. In 1948, he turned the Post over to his daughter's husband, Philip Graham, who built the Washington Post Co. into a profitable enterprise by acquiring radio and television stations, Newsweek magazine and, in 1955, the Post's only remaining morning rival, the Washington Times-Herald.

While the Washington Post Co. was thriving, though, the Post itself was just meandering along, shaking up few people and trying to get by on a shoestring. One reporter remembers being forbidden by a city editor from covering a major story in 1959 because it would have involved a $5 taxi fare. (He finally worked out a compromise—borrowing the city editor's car.)

Mr. Graham shot himself to death in 1963, and his widow, then 46 years old, took over the corporation and the paper. She soon set out to hire newspapermen who would make her paper great. Her major move came in 1965 when she hired as managing editor Benjamin Crowninshield Bradlee, Newsweek's Washington bureau chief who is as complex and controversial as the Post itself.

Mr. Bradlee, a gruff but witty and debonair man who looks rather like the Hollywood version of an international jewel thief, was given carte blanche to change the paper. "This was the great thing that happened to

the Post," asserts one former editor. "Mrs. Graham had
the guts to go out and redo the entire editorial side. Of
course, Bradlee had been pounding on her door anyway
for nine million years saying 'Why don't you let me be
your editor?' "

Mr. Bradlee proceeded to hire away a stream of
big-name reporters from other papers and to encourage
his staff to write controversial and probing pieces. He
offered top salaries—the minimum after four years on
the Post will rise to $15,000 this winter, and Mr. Bradlee
maintains that "good reporters have got to make at
least $20,000." And he offered an exciting forum. "The
Post is on every breakfast table (of the influential people) in Washington," notes Julius Duscha, director of
the Washington Journalism Center.

Before long, the Post was the most appetizing (or,
for some, unappetizing) thing on the table. Its writing
became sprightlier, its stories meatier. Its news became
more informative, its editorials more authoritative. The
paper became interesting, Washingtonians say. (An example: Until 1967, the Post's Pentagon correspondent
was a Naval Reserve officer who doubled as a columnist
for a Navy magazine. In the past year, by contrast, Post
Pentagon reporters have done a series of exposes, including revelations of the huge cost overruns on defense
contracts.)

Mr. Bradlee continued to make changes. In 1968, he
was named executive editor and subsequently three top
newsmen were brought in to help carry the load. Eugene C. Patterson, a Pulitzer Prize winner who was editor of the Atlanta Constitution, was named managing
editor of the Post. Philip Geyelin (pronounced JAY-lin),
long the State Department correspondent for The Wall
Street Journal, was named editor of the editorial pages,
and Ben H. Bagdikian, a free lance and well-known
critic of newspapers, was named national editor.

The appointment of Mr. Bagdikian was the most surprising. In 1967, he had written a sharply critical appraisal of the Post for the Columbia Journalism Review, concluding that the Evening Star "is generally regarded as more reliable by members of Congress and most of the working press." Two years later, he recalls, "Bradlee called me up and told me, 'Okay, you've been saying what's wrong with the Post, why don't you do something about it?'" The challenge was irresistible, Mr. Bagdikian says, so he signed on.

Mr. Bagdikian says he hasn't solved the problems he wrote about. The Post needed "a good drill sergeant," he said, and better news judgment. Mr. Bagdikian admits it still lacks the sergeant—there are many fiefdoms on the paper and they lack coordination—and he admits the news judgment still leaves something to be desired. "I called for a much more orderly process, and we've still got a good deal to go in that direction," he maintains. "The problem is how to achieve the order without suppressing the spontaneity. The Post is still a reporter's paper."

On occasion, two Post reporters from different departments will show up to cover the same event, and they argue on the spot over who will get the honors. The local, national, foreign, social and business staffs are highly competitive, and each is loyal to the division head. The in-fighting is said to be fierce. "The Post is even a worse snakepit than the New York Times," declares a news executive with close ties to both dailies. Many reporters feel compelled to tie themselves to a particular editor, who can lobby in their behalf with Mr. Bradlee. When a metropolitan editor was recently transferred to another position, several of his reporters made job inquiries with the Star.

"Ben (Bradlee) went out and tried to hire the best staff you could get without any thought of what you do with the staff when you get it," contends Walter Pincus, a top Post reporter who became disenchanted and quit a year ago. "You don't go on running the paper in the same way."

Other critics contend that the paper lacks long-term planning because Mr. Bradlee, the top editor, would rather spend his time getting involved in the day-to-day operation. Mr. Bradlee concedes he wants to stay involved.

"My great despair in life is that I'm going to be Peter-principled out of the news conference" (the daily meeting when editors decide what to run, and where). "Jesus, I'm only 48. I was a pretty good reporter, and that's what I like." Mr. Bradlee's office is on the news floor of the Post's cramped seven-story downtown headquarters, which is now undergoing a $25 million expansion, and he maintains a camaraderie with the staff; he has been known to toss a football around the newsroom with reporters, for instance, something that would be very, very unlikely to happen at the New York Times.

While Mr. Bradlee's concern for the present rather than the future upsets some persons, it obviously impresses others. Haynes Johnson, a Post reporter, says, "This is the best side of the Post—the editors care." He says that "the night of the demonstrations during last November's moratorium, I ran into Ben Bradlee getting gassed at one corner, and on the next corner I ran into Phil Geyelin getting gassed."

Mr. Geyelin, a 47-year-old Yale graduate who seems even more debonair and Ivy League than Mr. Bradlee, has made the Post's editorial pages as interesting and informative as anything in the paper. He turned the paper sharply against the Vietnam war when he took the job two years ago, and he and his eight-man staff of editorial writers continue sharp attacks on the Administration despite criticism.

"One doesn't want it said five years from now that the Washington Post was either asleep or frightened if in fact the Nixon Administration is beginning a calculated campaign for controls on freedom of the press," he declares. Under him Post editorials have become long and stimulating, but rarely pontifical. The editorials often contain fresh reporting.

"People more or less know how you'll come out, so there's no reason for them to read an editorial unless they'll learn something," he says, in explaining the value he puts on reporting. Also, he says, "We want to argue our case with some evidence." Besides attacking itself on occasion, the Post sometimes runs editorials headed "F.Y.I." in which certain practices of the paper and the profession—sometimes sloppy or unsavory practices—are explained to the readers.

Mr. Geyelin won a Pulitzer Prize for his efforts earlier this year.

Mr. Geyelin and Mr. Bradlee are given almost complete freedom by Mrs. Graham to run the paper as they choose. "I wouldn't describe this as a perfectly orderly organization," she says. "It has a certain sloppiness that has both virtues and faults. Ben and Phil are just very nice about talking to me and consulting me."

One place Mrs. Graham does interfere, however, is in the women's pages. Post society reporters are at almost every important party in Washington—except those thrown by Mrs. Graham. Her parties are off limits to the working press. "And they're rather the most important parties around here," asserts Mr. Bradlee. "She collects a better group of more significant in-the-news people." Though the press isn't allowed, Mrs. Graham does pass on lots of news that she picks up at her parties, Mr. Bradlee discloses.

The women's pages don't lack for news. On more than one occasion, they have contained the most impor-

tant story of the day. The Post, for instance, was the
first paper in the nation to print rumors of the retirement of Speaker John McCormack—on page three of
the women's section, since the rumors had circulated at
a party. The section, known since January 1969 as the
Style section, was designed to contain more sociology
and less gossip, but of late the emphasis has switched
back to gossip.

The most controversial feature of the Style section
is a column by 41-year-old Nicholas Von Hoffman that
appears every Monday, Wednesday and Friday. He is
the apostle of the growing movement toward activist
journalism, and there is nothing he will not attack. He
was given the column because of his tendency to be an
advocate as a reporter. In an introduction to a collec-
tion of Von Hoffman columns, Mr. Bradlee describes
how reporter Von Hoffman covered James Meredith's
march across Mississippi in 1966:

"His files would inevitably start with a paragraph
or two of reeking, local sociology—two red-neck mean-
ies relieving themselves against the cinderblock wall of
some filling station at the baked crossroads of nowhere.
The scene-setter would inevitably be followed by some
vintage vernacular, challenging an editor's standards of
taste. But if Meredith's name appeared in the copy, it
was an accident."

In his column, Mr. Von Hoffman has gone after
everyone from doctors (more interested in billing machines than medicine) to lawyers ("Squeeze, Squeeze,
Chisel and Gouge") to TV newscasters ("those Alpo
Dog Food salesmen who read the Associated Press wire
copy on the air.") It was he who attacked fellow columnist Joseph Alsop as an "old screech owl of war" and
Mr. Von Hoffman, in turn, has been attacked by Mr.
Geyelin in an editorial for one of his columns.

Mr. Von Hoffman considers his mission as "kicking

people in the ass in the hope that's the quickest way to reach their brains." Mrs. Graham says simply, "I think he's tremendously skilled—and like a lot of very talented people he enjoys outraging."

Mrs. Graham and the editors stand by the staff completely. The Indian embassy in Washington regularly complained about the stories written by Bernard Nossiter from there, but the editors withheld the complaints from him. An investigative series by Leonard Downie is said to have cost the paper a quarter of a million dollars in lost advertising from saving and loan associations, but no one at the Post complained to him.

Mr. Bradlee says that he used to get calls at one and two in the morning relaying messages of displeasure from President Johnson. "He used to say to Bill Moyers, 'You call that Ben Bradlee and tell him he's full of crap.' " Mr. Bradlee's sleep, but not his policy, was affected by the calls. Mrs. Graham says the Nixon Administration is different. "It has a policy I don't like of being silently angry," she says.

Mrs. Graham has many friends in the capital, but they are just as likely to be attacked in the Post as anyone else. "She's constantly embarrassed, but she never complains," a former Post editor says. Mrs. Graham herself says, "It's a little bit awkward when your friends are attacked, but it's essential to keep your personal feelings out of the paper. You hope the reporters don't know who your friends are."

—STANFORD N. SESSER

1970

Chicago Tribune

THE Chicago Tribune is not part of the Eastern liberal establishment press.

But that's one of the few things you can say for sure about the morning Tribune. You could say, as a survey of 180 newspaper editors found last year, that the Tribune is the "least fair" of 26 big-city newspapers. On the other hand, you could say, as another survey of 132 publishers found last year, that the Tribune is the nation's ninth best newspaper.

You could say that the conservative Republican paper is drifting toward the political middle; it broke tradition and endorsed a liberal Democrat for alderman in 1969 and another for Congressman. No, says Don Rose, a publicist for radical and civil rights groups, "you can't say the Tribune has gotten more liberal."

But you can say, says Mr. Rose, that the Tribune "has gotten more fair." No, say others, you can't say that, because the paper regularly convicts leftists before they have come to trial. For instance, editorials have flatly accused Angela Davis before her trial of being a "gun moll" and of "becoming weapons procurer and purveyor in an assault on the courts and the law."

What you can definitely say is that the Chicago Tribune today is not quite the Tribune of old. It is changing. But, as the conflicting comments indicate, the extent is open to dispute. And while observers argue

over how much it is changing, the staff argues over how
much the paper should change.

For the venerable Tribune, which fought some famous fights during the first half of this century under
the editorship of flamboyant Col. Robert R. McCormick,
is today involved in two of its biggest battles ever: it is
fighting among itself about where it should be headed,
and it is fighting with the Chicago Sun-Times to make
sure that, wherever it's headed, there will be an audience waiting for it.

The dispute within the paper is much like that on
many publications—a yearning for change by younger
staff members and a clinging to the old values by their
elders. What makes this fight different at the Trib is
that the old values on that newspaper seemed to many
to blatantly reject fairness as a desired quality in news
stories. "The Tribune used to be a good, strong, unfair
voice of conservatism. Some of the old guard didn't even
know what fairness was. The new guard does," says
Clarence Petersen, the radio and TV editor and one of
the most articulate of the new guarders.

The new guard doesn't ask that the paper change
its politics, merely that it be responsible. "I would like
to see the Tribune become a good, strong, fair voice of
conservatism," Mr. Petersen says.

Similarly, the new guard thinks the paper should
be more cognizant of news and views of blacks, who now
constitute nearly 40% of Chicago's population. The old
guard thinks instead that the paper's first responsibility is to its faithful following of older, conservative,
white Midwesterners in the four-state area from Mil-
waukee to Indianapolis and from Peoria to Grand Rap-
ids that the Tribune majestically includes in "Chicago-
land."

Tribune executives acknowledge that the paper
must change. The dilemma, they say, is that the paper

can ill afford to lose its faithful following, but neither
can it afford not to woo the blacks and young whites
who have so far shunned it as bland and biased. This is
a delicate balancing act, and, at the moment, it isn't
going well. "We are changing too fast for our older readers and maybe not fast enough for new readers," says
Mr. Petersen, the radio-TV editor.

Indeed, Tribune circulation is going downhill. With
weekday sales of 767,000 copies and Sunday circulation
of slightly more than one million, the Tribune is the nation's fifth largest newspaper and the largest daily published in an inland city. Yet these figures are down considerably from circulation of more than one million
weekdays and 1.6 million on Sunday in the paper's hey-
day in the late 1940s.

The current circulation comfortably exceeds that of
Field Enterprises' Sun-Times, the lively morning tabloid
that is bought by 536,000 persons on weekdays and
709,000 on Sundays. But the gap is narrowing. During
the past five years, the Sun-Times' weekday sales
slipped 2,000—but the Tribune's fell 73,000. In the same
period, the Sun-Times Sunday circulation rose 16,000
while Tribune Sunday sales fell a whopping 162,000. For
several years the Sun-Times has outsold the Tribune in
Chicago proper, and now the Field paper is making in-
roads in the city's predominately white, middle-class
suburbs, which have long been the Tribune's traditional
stronghold.

"If we continue to accept such losses, we'll be in
trouble," concedes Charles A. Corcoran, Tribune circulation director. But, he adds, "I think we've bottomed
out. I don't look for any dramatic gains, but I do expect
a series of short, consistent gains."

Neither the Tribune nor its parent, the Tribune Co.,
reports financial figures, and H. F. Grumhaus, publisher of the paper and president of the company, will

say only that revenues of the paper alone declined in 1970 to $119 million from $124 million in 1969. He blames the decline on a drop in advertising, though the Tribune still has more advertising revenue than the other three major Chicago dailies combined. Besides owning the Tribune, the Tribune Co. publishes the afternoon Chicago Today (formerly called Chicago's American), the New York News (which has the largest circulation of any newspaper in the U.S.) and five Florida dailies. It also owns several television and radio stations and two newsprint mills in Canada.

Ironically, while its financial fortunes have faded, the Tribune has become a better newspaper—though how much better can cause an argument between most any two Tribune readers. Physically, the paper has become more modern. It has dropped hard-to-read headlines of all capital letters. It has restyled its sports pages and several Sunday sections adopting breezy layouts and a six-column format. Eventually, editor Clayton Kirkpatrick, a 33-year veteran at the paper, hopes to scrap the traditional, constricting eight-column format throughout the paper.

Ideologically, it has also become easier for more readers to read. Views that differ from its own are creeping into its pages; while conservative syndicated columnists William S. White and S. I. Hayakawa appear on Sunday, so, too, does liberal columnist Clayton Fritchey. A new Sunday section, Perspective—which Sunday editor Walter Simmons calls "at least 10 years overdue"—runs articles by such disparate contributors as J. Edgar Hoover and Rep. Shirley Chisholm and recently reprinted a piece on racially discriminatory suburban zoning laws from left-leaning Nation magazine.

The paper has added youth-oriented features—including the comic strips "Doonesbury" and "Broom-Hilda," which Mr. Kirkpatrick describes as "new and with it"—and women's page editors have run stories sympathetic to abortion law reform and to women's lib. (But male editors assigned a man to cover last August's "Women Strike for Women," and the resulting story sneered at the demonstration as "a flop.")

The paper has also gone from prudish to prim. It no longer bars sex novels such as "Tropic of Cancer," "The Carpetbaggers" and "Candy" from its list of best-selling books. Recently it ran a friendly piece on the author of "The Sensuous Woman." All this is a far cry from the Sunday three years ago when the Tribune destroyed 1.1 million copies of its book supplement, Book World, because a review of "The Naked Ape" stated that "the human male and not the gorilla possesses the largest penis of all primates."

This expanded and fairer coverage of Chicago and the world is being written by an expanded and fairer staff. While the paper hasn't won a Pulitzer Prize since 1962, many of its 530 editorial staffers are considered to be top-rank journalists. General-assignment reporters' salaries range up to $300 a week, among the highest in the Midwest, so the paper has little trouble attracting good and potentially good journalists. The biggest drawback in hiring, editors say, is the paper's reputation as an unfair, right-wing publication carrying on the policies of Col. McCormick, who died in 1955.

That view is hammered into Chicago residents at a young age. "Kids learn to hate the Tribune from their teachers," says Mr. Petersen. "In grammar and high school, they're told the Tribune is unfair, reactionary and slants the news." That infuriates some Tribune editors. "Most of the things people know about the Tribune aren't so—and weren't even when they attained currency," insists editor Kirkpatrick.

But right-wing views are still found throughout the paper, sometimes in unusual places. Bob Markus, a sports columnist, last spring concluded a column on brawls among Chicago Cub fans by saying:

"How can you control rebellion on the local level when the Supreme Court of the U.S., forgetting that justice is a two-way street, disregarding the rights and wishes of the vast majority of law-abiding Americans, hands down decisions that give the criminal element virtual license to kill, rape, and pillage? How can you stop riots in the baseball park when the U.S. Senate twice thwarts the President of the U.S. when he attempts to restore a sane balance to the high court?"

And the front page sometimes displays cartoons of the type that most papers reserve for their editorial pages. The cartoons usually pillory Communists, Democrats or unions. A cartoon last Thanksgiving showed a huge turkey labeled "labor demands" pecking at a tiny, frightened man labeled "taxpayer." Read the caption: "Gobble! Gobble!"

To avoid unnecessarily alienating some of the young, the paper recently dropped its front page slogan "the American paper for Americans." But it still pushes patriotism on page one by printing a sketch of the American flag in the upper lefthand corner. And each day inside the paper there's a photo of a flag flying at a home or business in the Chicago area. The paper offers readers three-foot-by-five-foot flags for $3.50, and it has sold 71,000 of them since 1961. It regards flag display as appropriate nearly anytime and anywhere. Columnist Robert Wiedrich recently wrote:

"Wearing Old Glory on a police uniform, a business suit, or for that matter, on your pajamas when you kneel in prayer for this country at night, is a good idea, especially in these times."

While flag-waving strikes even the paper's detractors as a harmless idiosyncrasy, critics say some other Tribune characteristics are far from harmless. They cite the papers' seemingly reflexive support of the police. When Richard J. Elrod, then assistant corporation counsel of Chicago, was partially paralyzed during an SDS Weatherman demonstration in the fall of 1969, a front-page story in the Tribune categorically stated he had been "hit on the head by a pipe-swinging demonstrator." Trial testimony subsequently disclosed that Mr. Elrod had hurt himself while tackling his alleged assailant, Brian Flanagan, who was acquitted—to the Tribune's disgust.

"The Tribune was remiss in assuming that Flanagan struck Elrod, and saying this without attribution," says editor Kirkpatrick.

And in 1969, after Chicago police raided a Black Panther headquarters and killed two Panthers, the Tribune published an exclusive photograph purporting to show holes from bullets fired from inside the flat— evidence that the Panthers had fired first. A close examination of the scene, however, showed that the "bullet holes" actually were rusty nail heads.

"It was a horrible mistake, a blot on my record," laments Mr. Kirkpatrick. "We relied on the cops' version, and perhaps we should have been more cautious."

The paper rarely sensationalizes crime and sex-scandal stories, as it and other Chicago papers regularly did during the Front Page era of Chicago journalism, but it does sensationalize stories involving drugs and crusades against drugs both hard and soft. When a 20-year-old girl was arrested here not long ago for growing marijuana in her apartment, the paper ran a mug shot of her and the caption: "Dope Suspect."

Such crusades could be expected on an editorial page, and, indeed, the Tribune editorial page is as zealous a page as any in America—though not so vituperative as in the old days when Col. McCormick used the page to personally attack his enemies. But the paper can still get pretty rough at times. A 1968 editorial charging that black student demonstrators at the University of Illinois "went ape" and "swung from chandeliers" struck some blacks as racist. And when Martin Luther King campaigned for racial justice in Chicago in 1966, the Tribune editorially accused him of "hot air" and "grandstanding," and its editor refused to see him. "I don't think Col. McCormick would have received him, and I didn't see why I should," recalls William D. Maxwell, then editor. "You can't talk to everyone who comes to town and has a press agent who asks you to see him." (But Mr. Kirkpatrick, who succeeded Mr. Maxwell two years ago, has met with black leaders several times and once ordered a lengthy news story and a favorable editorial about a local black college president whose ouster the Tribune had previously sought.)

Most editorials are directed by George Morgenstern, the 64-year-old editor of the editorial page. Mr. Morgenstern is one of the old guard's most influential members, a man who got his views and learned his trade at Col. McCormick's knee.

Mr. Morgenstern's page dislikes the United Nations ("this futile and increasingly mischevious organization"), is strongly anti-Soviet and is hawkish on the war. However, because of what Mr. Kirkpatrick calls "diminishing interest" in the war among readers, the Tribune has stopped sending Chicago-area servicemen in Vietnam a free color photo of their families at Christmas.

Though it's clearly a Republican paper, the Tribune has long gotten along well with the city's strong Democratic machine. It backed Richard J. Daley when he ran for reelection as mayor in 1967, and it has few quarrels with his administration. "Daley has been a good mayor," says Mr. Morgenstern. "Generally he has been a source for stability in this city. We have some reservations about him because he keeps padding the payroll and kicking up the property taxes."

The editorial page is clearly worried about where this country is headed. Walter Trohan, a semi-retired Washington correspondent who contributes a regular column, devoted a recent column to "whether or not free governments have generally perished not so much by disruption from without as by vote of the people." This is a danger in the U.S., he went on, judging by the "known fact that the policies of the government today, whether Republican or Democratic, are closer to the 1932 platform of the Communist Party than they are to either of their own party platforms in that critical year."

Embarrassed by such extremism, some new guarders at the Tribune would like to see the Tribune drop the columns of Mr. Trohan and of semi-retired correspondent Willard Edwards, a long-time anti-Communist crusader who once helped an obscure Congressman named Richard Nixon prepare a case against Alger Hiss. So far, these new guarders have succeeded only in having the columns switched from regular news pages to the editorial page.

But if the Tribune can be zealous in causes that upset the new guarders, so, too, can it be zealous in causes they support. The paper has taken a strong interest in cleaning up air and water pollution, and environment editor Casey Bukro regularly names companies—including major advertisers—that he says pollute Lake Michigan and the other Great Lakes.

"The Tribune has taken good stands on pollution and reform of the state constitution," says Leon Despres, a Chicago alderman and long-time critic of the Tribune. "But on social issues it has exerted a very blighting, benighted, backward influence." David Halvorsen, the new guard city editor, all but agrees. "The

Tribune is without peer in covering establishment news —the school board, city hall, Springfield (the legislature)," he says. "But we don't always seem to get into the ballgame on social issues at the grass roots level."

Mr. Halvorsen promises the Tribune will do better in these areas, and regular readers say they have seen some change even in recent weeks. Mr. Halvorsen also acknowledged that "we aren't the liveliest paper in town," and he promises the Tribune will brighten up.

The paper is indeed filled with dry, uninspired writing that reads as if it had been turned out by a humorless computer. One reason may be the Tribune's unusual requirement that reporters turn in 10 copies of each story they write. This enables many editors to check the story for accuracy, but the need to please so many critics discourages the writers from departing from safe stylistic norms.

Mr. Halvorsen, a 38-year-old who has been city editor since October, says it is sometimes frustrating to be a new guarder, but insiders say that lately he and his troops have been winning at least as many battles as they lose. A typical clash between the two factions took place last year after he assigned a story on Eva Jefferson, Northwestern University's first black president of the student body. Old guarder Tom W. Moore, then managing editor, killed it on the ground Miss Jefferson had already received too much favorable publicity.

But on Jan. 1, Mr. Moore was shifted to night managing editor and new guarder Russell Freeburg was named managing editor. Two days later, by coincidence or not, another profile of Miss Jefferson surfaced in the Sunday magazine section, a new guard stronghold.

—A. KENT MACDOUGALL

1971

E.J. Van Nostrand:
Easygoing Editor

IT'S five o'clock in the afternoon and E. J. Van Nostrand has just put out the day's edition of the Creston News-Advertiser. As he relaxes over a beer at Berning's Cafe, Dr. John Hoyt comes over to tell him about a new radiation treatment facility being installed at the local hospital. C. C. Houghton, the banker, joins the group and puts in a plug for coverage of the Creston Musicale series. People smile and wave as they pass outside the restaurant's plate-glass window.

Mr. Van Nostrand, the News-Advertiser's lean, 61-year-old editor and publisher, says he knows just about everyone in this southwest Iowa farm town of 8,300 residents. That's good, he adds, because it helps him fill his Monday-through-Saturday newspaper with the local news that people here want to read.

But knowing everybody also can have its drawbacks for a newsman, the editor concedes. "When you've got to deal constantly with the people you write about, it isn't easy to be too critical," he says. "In a town like this, it helps to avoid getting personal about issues and to emphasize the good side of things whenever you can."

Mr. Van Nostrand's situation isn't unique. As long

as there have been newspapers, reporters and editors have had to balance the risk of offending their news sources against their professional duty to keep the public informed.

The way Mr. Van Nostrand has resolved this conflict isn't new, either. More than 60 years ago editor Warren G. Harding of the Marion, Ohio, Star, circulated a memo advising his news staff to "bring out the good and never needlessly hurt the feelings of anyone." Summed up the only newspaper editor who ever became President of the U.S.: "Boost, don't knock."

Lately, however, such thinking has come under increasing attack from those who contend that the press should take a more incisive look at the events it covers and be less protective of so-called Establishment figures. To date, most of this criticism has been directed at the way big city papers report on such hotly controversial subjects as the war in Vietnam, black power, student militancy and national politics. But many observers say that the same sort of scrutiny might well be directed at small-town papers' coverage of their local scenes.

Small papers don't have the scope of their bigger counterparts, of course, but they can be potent figures in their own backyards. In more than a quarter of the 435 Congressional districts in the U.S., for instance, the largest newspaper has a circulation of less then 25,000. In addition, the small-town daily usually doesn't face the news competition from radio and television that metropolitan newspapers do. This means it often is the small-town resident's sole source of extensive information about local matters.

And, it's asserted, the typical small-town editor doesn't live up to his popular image as a crusader. "Whatever problems big city papers have in reporting local issues in a hard-hitting way are magnified several

times in the small-town press," says Charles E. Hood Jr.
of the University of Montana journalism faculty, a close
student of small dailies. "Small-town papers typically
are hampered by local provincial attitudes and a shortage of qualified people. In some towns, the major issues
aren't even raised in the local press."

Jack Gillard, who as state editor of the Des Moines
Register leafs through dozens of small newspapers each
day, agrees. "The distressing thing is their overriding
concern about their town's image," he says. "When we
uncover a small town controversy, the local editor usually is madder at us for writing about the problem than
he is about the problem itself."

Mr. Van Nostrand, who has headed the News-Advertiser since 1946 and has been a small-town newsman since graduating from Monmouth College in Illinois in 1929, takes issue with the harsher critics of the
small-town press. "You just antagonize people in a
small town if you come on too strong," he says. "The
big-city editor is like the farmer who has to hit his mule
over the head with a two-by-four to get him to pay attention. There's no need for that here."

No one has ever accused the News-Advertiser of ig-
noring the Creston scene. Unlike the many small-town
papers that regularly fill their pages with stories supplied by wire services and feature syndicates, the News-
Advertiser's daily editions of six to 16 pages are almost
totally devoted to Creston doings. It has won a number
of awards for its local coverage.

The paper is a member of Associated Press but uses
only a half-dozen or so AP stories a day, most of them
from elsewhere in Iowa. National and international
news is almost totally absent; editor Van Nostrand believes that local people get all that they want from the
Des Moines Register, which circulates widely in town,

and from network television (there is no local television and just one local radio station).

The News-Advertiser operates with a full-time news staff of three. Managing editor is Charles Kelly, a stocky, 60-year-old bachelor who came to Creston in 1946, shortly before Mr. Van Nostrand. Mr. Kelly never went to college: he got his experience by working on a number of other small dailies. At the News-Advertiser he writes stories, edits AP wire copy and the stories of his staff, writes headlines and handles page layouts.

The other two staffers had no newspaper experience when they came to work for the News-Advertiser. Sports editor Max Sandeman, a confessed "sports nut," was working in a local clothing store when he joined the paper in 1947. Mrs. Mildred Hoskinson, a tall, gray-haired former schoolteacher, became society writer 12 years ago to supplement the income of her husband, a retired farmer.

The News-Advertiser isn't making any of its staff wealthy. Mr. Van Nostrand won't disclose his salary, but he and his wife, Virginia, live in a rather modest frame house (their one child, a son, is grown and works as a newspaperman in Vancouver, Wash.). Managing editor Kelly makes $125 for a 48-hour week. Sports editor Sandeman, a father of four, manages the local golf club on the side to help make ends meet.

Yet all say they like their jobs, especially the latitude they are given to comment on their specialties or exercise their literary talents. Mr. Sandeman's pride and joy is his twice-weekly column, "Lookin' Them Over," a mixture of miscellaneous local sports news and opinions ("After two years with an undefeated football team plus the always successful Cardinal Relays, it is hard to see how a school's athletic fund could get so far behind . . .").

Mrs. Hoskinson's weekly column is called "Fact and

Fancy." In it she writes poetry, carries poetic efforts by subscribers ("I never expected to live to 93/ But that is what has happened to me") and inserts an occasional bit of her own philosophy. "One of the nicest things about being an adult," she recently wrote, "is not having to buy your shoes a size too large because you expect to grow out of them before you wear them out if you don't."

Mr. Van Nostrand also has a column, a chatty affair called "Visiting With Neighbors," which runs Saturdays. In addition, he writes five editorials a week (some small-town papers don't even carry editorials) and frequent news stories and also sells ads when his two ad salesmen aren't available. Among the local groups he covers regularly are the City Planning Commission, Chamber of Commerce and Creston College. It's easy for him to do this because he is a member of the Planning Commission, a past president of the Chamber of Commerce and a trustee of the college, a two-year public institution.

Journalism textbooks frown on newsmen writing about events or groups in which they participate; they recommend that reporters play the role of disinterested observers. Mr. Van Nostrand says that this idea is "fine in theory" and concedes that "a lot of groups want to get us involved because they think it will get them more publicity in the paper." But he explains apologetically that "papers like ours just don't have enough manpower," to permit complete separation of roles. "I figure that as long as I'm there, I might as well write something, too," he says.

The paper's manpower shortage means the News-Advertiser rarely has a chance to investigate many local problems. Mr. Van Nostrand says he would like to see his paper taking a closer look at the city's sewage system and the quality of street paving, both of which he considers poor. There is also a need for more youth activities and more doctors in Creston, he says. To give better coverage to these matters, Mr. Van Nostrand says he has considered hiring another reporter but decided against it. "If I gave Kelly more people, he wouldn't know how to assign them," he says with a laugh. "He likes to do everything himself."

Mr. Van Nostrand isn't apologetic about his civic boosterism, however. He cites with pride the fact that Creston's population has climbed to its current 8,300 from 7,700 in 1960, "in a period when a lot of other small towns haven't been doing too well." New industry is the key to this growth, he says; it has helped the town build a new hospital and a new campus for Creston College over the past few years.

The News-Advertiser has also benefited from Creston's prosperity. Its circulation now stands at 6,300, an all-time high. Three years ago it moved into a new office on Adams Street, the town's main thoroughfare. Mr. Van Nostrand has an ownership interest in the paper, which is operated as a subsidiary of Shaw Newspapers Inc., a Midwestern chain. He worked on a Shaw paper in Newton, Iowa, before being transferred to Creston.

Mr. Van Nostrand's daily round reflects his deep involvement in local affairs. On one recent day he spent most of his morning at a meeting of the Chamber of Commerce's Task Force on Downtown Development, a group of local business and professional men charged with looking into ways to refurbish the town's central shopping district. (He later wrote an account of the meeting for his paper.)

He spent several hours that afternoon at a local farm judging a bean-growing contest for the Chamber. He volunteered for the assignment "because it's good to keep up contacts with the farmers—they're awfully important, too."

Mr. Van Nostrand has always been wary of throwing his weight around in editorials—an attitude that critics might attribute, at least in part, to his reluctance to offend. In 1947, shortly after he came to town, he decided that Creston needed a swimming pool. Instead of saying so editorially, he promoted the idea through a News-Advertiser float in a Fourth of July parade. He later worked behind the scenes for passage of the bond issue that enabled the pool to be built.

"I was new, and I didn't want to seem bossy," he says in explaining why he didn't editorialize in support of the project.

Mr. Van Nostrand has stuck to that philosophy. Newspaper editorials traditionally support or oppose things—"I don't know of anyone who's in a better position to be an authority on his community than the local editor," says John Stempel, former head of the Indiana University journalism department—but Mr. Van Nostrand's editorials rarely do. Mostly, they simply set down the pros and cons of an issue. This reluctance to take a stand extends to the least controversial of matters. Commenting on a large voter turnout at a recent school board election, he wrote that "generally speaking, it is considered desirable to have a good turnout at the school election polls."

The editor has even avoided coming out against proposals he has personally opposed. A few years ago, for instance, he felt that a $300,000 bond issue to build a railroad underpass downtown was an extravagance, but he didn't oppose it because it was the brainchild of his friend, city attorney William McLaughlin. "It was close to Bill's heart, and he'd done a good job for the city," he says. (The bond issue lost anyway.)

Mr. Van Nostrand is somewhat more forthright in his handling of the News-Advertiser's news columns. He tries hard not to let advertisers influence news stories, although he does provide free publicity for movies at the local theater and for new model cars at local dealerships, all of which advertise regularly. And he insists that criminal violations by adults in town will be reported in his paper no matter who the offender is.

But even when faced with the crudest sort of pressure—one man recently offered the paper $50 in advertising if a story about his arrest for speeding were suppressed—he still tries to be diplomatic. "We explain our policies to anyone who wants to know them," he says. "Usually people agree with us once we do that."

Stories that might prove embarrassing to local officials often are softened or avoided, however. Last March a Creston man picked up his party-line telephone and overheard two young men planning a break-in that night at a store in Creston. The man notified the store's owner, who in turn notified police.

Despite the warning, the break-in took place on schedule and $300 in merchandise was stolen. The police told the outraged store owner that they had assigned a man to watch his establishment but he had left early because he got cold.

The News-Advertiser reported the break-in but not the advance tip. That didn't get into print until five days after the burglary and long after it had been reported by the local radio station. Even then, the paper never editorially criticized the police for their apparent neglect of duty.

Mr. Van Nostrand still isn't altogether sure that the police should be criticized because of the incident. "Maybe we missed the boat on that one, but it does get awfully cold here in March," he says.

—DAN ROTTENBERG

1969

William Loeb:

Irascible Publisher

TO Publisher William Loeb, former president Eisenhower was "dopey Dwight," Republican Sen. Mar-
garet Chase Smith of Maine is "Moscow Maggie" and
Martin Luther King was "a complete pious fraud" who,
like President John Kennedy and Sen. Robert Kennedy,
brought on his own death by encouraging violence.

Such opinions are the daily diet of the 60,000 readers of Mr. Loeb's Manchester Union Leader, New Hampshire's only statewide newspaper. The publisher puts his
invective where nobody can miss it, in signed editorials
on the front page. And he embellishes these with such
headlines as "Teddy Is Just Plain Stupid," which appeared over a fulmination against Sen. Edward Kennedy.

Such blasts have made Mr. Loeb and his main
paper (he owns three others) violently controversial.
Critics ranging from politicians to Roman Catholic
priests frequently buy ads, often on the front page, to
answer him; at times nearly all the front-page space not
occupied by Loeb editorials denouncing various people
and organizations is taken up by ads denouncing Mr.
Loeb.

The publisher is frequently embroiled in lawsuits,

either as plaintiff or defendant; even his mother once
sued him, seeking control of his papers (the case was
settled out of court). Several committees of state politicians, businessmen and clergymen have been formed
specifically to combat him. One, which calls itself
Friends of Fair Journalism, is studying the possibility
of starting a competing paper.

But even critics concede Mr. Loeb is influential.
How much so is in dispute, as the publisher has lost
some big fights. Barry Goldwater lost the 1964 state Republican Presidential primary despite a strong Loeb endorsement, and Sen. Eugene J. McCarthy polled a huge
vote in this year's Democratic primary despite Loeb editorials calling him a "skunk" and his followers "mur-
derers" whose dovish stand was endangering the lives of
American fighting men in Vietnam.

But Mr. Loeb also has built unknowns into serious
contenders for high office. Retired Air Force Brig. Gen.
Harrison R. Thyng, a Vietnam hawk, scored a stunning
upset in the 1966 GOP Senatorial primary after a Loeb
aide persuaded him to run. (He lost the general election, though, to Democrat Thomas J. McIntyre, who
called Mr. Loeb's paper a "malignant cancer in the society of New Hampshire.")

Politicians add that fear of Mr. Loeb's pen has kept
many potential candidates from seeking office. Bill
Johnson, a Republican state legislator, says several
"highly qualified" Republicans chose not to run for
Senator in 1966 for that reason. A prominent Democrat
comments: "We've got a lot of bright young attorneys
who just don't want to face his vendettas." ("They must
be extremely tender characters," replies Mr. Loeb.)

Mr. Loeb is often cited as the main reason that New
Hampshire is the only state without either an income or
a sales tax. "It's a monumental task to advocate a tax
reform in this state, because you can't overcome the in-

fluence of the Manchester paper," complains Eugene Stuckoff, a Concord attorney.

What influence Mr. Loeb will have on the current election remains to be seen. As frequently happens he has become an issue in it himself. Democratic Gov. John W. King, now running for the Senate, has charged that his Republican opponent, Sen. Norris Cotton, "will do (Mr. Loeb's) paper's bidding," adding: "New Hampshire needs a completely independent Senator . . . unbeholden to the Union Leader."

"Whenever they (politicians) haven't got a good issue, they try to make one of me," retorts Mr. Loeb. During the recent uproar over the nomination of Abe Fortas as Chief Justice, the publisher attacked Gov. King for supporting Mr. Fortas, charging the governor was "making it easier for every smut peddler in the country." In the Presidential race, Mr. Loeb backs Richard Nixon, whom he says he considers a friend, though he worries that "Dick still has to convince people he isn't anti-labor."

A surprising worry for a self-styled "Teddy Roosevelt conservative" and ardent admirer of the late Sen. Joseph R. McCarthy? Perhaps—but Mr. Loeb has long been a staunch supporter of trade unions, and in particular of the Teamsters and their jailed leader, Jimmy Hoffa ("a guy with great integrity"). Indeed, his papers are in debt to the Teamsters for loans of over $2 million.

Support of labor is only one of a bundle of seeming contradictions about Mr. Loeb. Though he owns four papers, he contends nobody should be allowed to own more than one. Though he called Nelson Rockefeller a "wife swapper" for divorcing his first wife and marrying a divorced woman, Mr. Loeb is himself divorced and married to a divorcee. He spent a night in a Vermont jail after being arrested on alienation-of-affection charges brought by his current wife's first husband. The suit was later dropped.

Though he is highly influential in New Hampshire, Mr. Loeb doesn't live in the state—a point not lost on his critics. He maintains a 100-acre estate in Pride's Crossing, Mass., and a home in Reno, Nev.

And though his acid tongue has not only infuriated enemies but embarrassed some of his allies, Mr. Loeb turns out in the course of a four-and-a-half-hour interview to be highly congenial and cordial in person. "I take the things I believe in very seriously but never take myself seriously," he says.

Some foes seem to take Mr. Loeb very seriously indeed; associates say his life has been threatened several times. Both the 62-year-old publisher and his 44-year-old second wife, Nackey Scripps, carry guns almost all the time; not surprisingly, Mr. Loeb is a foe of all gun-control legislation. The family's Jeep station wagon is loaded with alarm devices to prevent tinkering. (It's also decorated with a front license plate, a gift from George Wallace, that reads "Governor's Staff—Stand Up for Alabama.")

But Mr. Loeb equally discusses the most sensitive matters. His attack on Gov. Rockefeller for a marital history similar to his own? "I wasn't running for President and he was." His nonresidency in New Hampshire? "If I could find a suitable place in New Hampshire, I'd live there." His mother's lawsuit? "Unfortunately, she was influenced by my first wife." His indulgence in the multiple newspaper ownership he says should be forbidden? "As long as it's permissible I'll own several papers, but I'm against the concept."

The publisher even implies the explosive opinions he voices in his editorials are to some extent conscious hyperbole. "I write strong editorials so they'll stick in people's minds," he says.

But he doesn't take anything back. After his description of Sen. Eugene McCarthy as a "skunk" raised a storm, he changed the characterization to "a skunk's skunk." And the assassinations of John and Robert Kennedy haven't softened his opinions of them or their brother, Edward Kennedy.

Mr. Loeb once was an acquaintance of Joseph Kennedy, the family's founding father, but a former associate of the publisher says he "despises the kids—I think he resents their success." Mr. Loeb himself says: "Frankly, I'm not fond of the beautiful people. I don't like the arrogance of the Kennedys."

At least one Kennedy—John—made it clear in public that he reciprocated Mr. Loeb's scorn. Incensed during the 1960 campaign by a Loeb charge that he didn't "understand communism," John Kennedy shouted at an election eve rally in Manchester that the Union Leader was "the most irresponsible newspaper in the country"—one of the few times the late President ever lost his temper in public.

(Pleased with the explosion he provoked on that occasion, Mr. Loeb recently recommended that Republican Vice Presidential candidate Spiro Agnew not call Hubert Humphrey "soft on communism" but instead try the "he doesn't understand communism" approach.)

Mr. Loeb's "Teddy Is Just Plain Stupid" editorial came last summer when Edward Kennedy made a speech criticizing U.S. policy in Vietnam. The editorial focused on the Senator's previous admission that he had once cheated on a college examination in Spanish.

"To cheat in a mathematics exam would be immoral," Mr. Loeb wrote, "but at least it would be understandable. But, Spanish is always the snap course. . . . If Kennedy is so stupid as not to be able to pass a Spanish examination, he is pretty badly off indeed." Asked what relevance this had to Vietnam policy, Mr. Loeb replies: "I just didn't want to see a buildup get started for Teddy."

At other times, Mr. Loeb has had a good deal to say about Vietnam. He favors escalation, including "the bombing of Haiphong off the map" and use of all force "necessary" to win.

He hits hard at other issues, as well as personalities, too—especially race. Mr. Loeb denies charges by Roy Wilkins, head of the National Association for the Advancement of Colored People, that he is a "racist." He points out that the Union Leader has a Negro columnist. He is George Schuyler, an ultraconservative.

But the publisher has opposed all civil rights bills for the last five years. He contends: "I just know what happens when you try to force people to get along with each other." In 1964, he served as chairman of a group called Coordinating Committee for Fundamental American Freedoms Inc. It ran ads in the Union Leader and other papers denouncing that year's civil rights act as a "blackjack" and organized letter-writing campaigns to Congressmen in an attempt to defeat it.

Several Senators, including Hubert Humphrey, called the Coordinating Committee a "front" for the Mississippi Sovereignty Commission, a state-supported segregationist agency. Mr. Loeb denies the charge but says the Mississippi agency did contribute money to his group after it was organized. He adds that he was unaware of this at the time but that "it wouldn't have made any difference" if he had known of it.

The Union Leader doesn't capitalize the word "Negro"; asked why, Mr. Loeb replies simply that it doesn't capitalize "white" either. But critics say this policy is an example of the way the publisher's biases influence not only the paper's editorial columns but its news content.

The critics say that Arthur Egan, the Union Leader's investigative reporter, frequently roams the country seeking information to discredit Jimmy Hoffa's convictions (Mr. Loeb denies a widespread rumor that the Teamsters Union pays for these trips). And the paper raised some eyebrows last month with its coverage of a group of 41 Catholic priests who accused Mr. Loeb in an ad of creating "a climate of fear, distrust and suspicion." An initial news story was devoted mostly to a recital of controversial activities the priests had been engaged in, mostly antiwar efforts; later stories strongly suggested the Bishop of New Hampshire should disavow the ad. Bishop Primeau eventually did say he had had nothing to do with it. (A few days ago, a group of 107 Protestant ministers ran an ad seconding the priests' ad.)

Critics fume most about the extent to which they feel the Union Leader plays down news about Mr. Loeb's opponents. A critic who studied the paper for a month before the 1964 New Hampshire Republican Presidential primary claimed it gave four times as much news space to Barry Goldwater's campaign as it did to Nelson Rockefeller's activities.

"We know the Union Leader will run our releases, but they'll usually be buried, and only the bad news will be highlighted," says an aide to one Republican politician whom Mr. Loeb has attacked. "The only way to counter Loeb is to buy front-page ads—so you end up paying him every time he hits you."

Some other targets of the paper have sought to counter Mr. Loeb by filing libel suits. In recent years, the Union Leader has paid a libel judgment of $99,000 to a Manchester nursery-home operator, settled out of court a suit by two Derry, N.H., women and made a number of corrections or apologies after other libel suits were threatened.

Mr. Loeb's friendliness toward the Teamsters and unions generally didn't prevent Boston publishers from labeling him a "strike-breaker" when he published a Boston edition of the Union Leader during a newspaper strike there last year. But the publisher has never slackened in his editorial support of unionism; for instance, he has long advocated repeal of the section of the Taft-Hartley Act that allows states to outlaw the union shop.

On his own paper, Mr. Loeb pays high salaries and frequently helps to defray medical bills and extraordinary expenses for employes ("He's a soft touch for anybody in trouble," says Mr. Finnegan, the editorial writer). The Union Leader in 1949 became one of the first newspapers to initiate a profit-sharing plan for employes, and the Loebs plan to leave control to employes when they die.

Even the publisher's critics concede he runs a good newspaper in some other ways. Its statewide coverage is unexcelled. Though Mr. Loeb has been a constant critic of the University of New Hampshire, a university official says the Union Leader is "the only paper that sends a reporter to the campus regularly." A harsh critic of Mr. Loeb adds that "in terms of sheer writing and reporting ability," the paper's chief political reporter, D. Frank O'Neil, is outstanding, though he says Mr. O'Neil "follows the (Loeb) party line."

Whatever treatment they may get in the news columns, opinions opposed to Mr. Loeb's can find an outlet in the Union Leader's letters column. The paper prints more than 100 letters a week—more than any other daily, its editors boast—and though most of the letters it gets have a right-wing flavor, the column is open to all shades of opinion.

—ALBERT R. HUNT

1968

Pravda:

The Kremlin's Voice

A ROUND the world, it was front page news: Nikita Khrushchev was dead.

But in Moscow, the death rated a mere 57 words in Pravda—nearly 48 hours after the event. To readers of Pravda, the world's leading Communist newspaper, the scant coverage really wasn't abnormal; it simply confirmed again that the deposed Soviet leader was still on the official blacklist.

News coverage that is strange or stale to Western eyes is standard fare in Pravda. For a typical lead front-page item one recent day, the paper carried a verbatim transcript of a government directive on farm irrigation. The same day, the paper featured inside a picture of three computer engineers stressing the need for increased industrial efficiency.

But Soviet citizens read Pravda with avid fascination. Unlike any Western newspaper, this principal organ of the Soviet Union's Communist Party is the rule book and source of current ideology for a whole nation. If you know how to read them, all those dry reports— like the belated handling of the Khrushchev death—are full of intriguing clues about what is really going on in Russia.

50

Dull as Pravda might seem to American readers, it is in many ways one of the world's most successful—and most profitable—publications. With a circulation of 9.3 million, Pravda has become the world's largest-selling daily newspaper. Circulation has soared 41% from the 6.6 million in 1965. The party paper has thus decidedly bypassed its closest competitor, the government paper Izvestia, which sells about 7 million copies a day.

This year Pravda expects to earn a profit that would make many publishers of far jazzier capitalist papers drool: $22 million, or more than 27% of sales. This despite a newsstand price of three kopeks (3.3 U.S. cents) and advertising revenues of zero.

Pravda (which means "truth" in Russian) is top priority reading for Westerners trying to detect shifts in Soviet policy—providing they know how to find the clues. In April each year, for instance, Pravda publishes a series of suggested slogans for May Day celebration banners and placards.

Last May Day's suggested slogans included: "Hail May 1, Day of International Solidarity of the Toilers" and "Proletarians of the World, Unite." This may sound innocuous enough. But when the Soviets are in a belligerent mood, slogans warn against "American imperialism" or "West German revanchism." Thus innocuous slogans can have real meaning.

This year's 60 suggested slogans treated the tries mildly. They seemed to treat Zionism as the biggest outside enemy and stressed Arab-Soviet solidarity.

"Our approach to stories is different from a paper like, say, The New York Times," says Serge Tsukasov, the youthful-looking 48-year-old managing editor. "We direct ourselves to problems, not to events."

Thus crime, catastrophe or celebrity news that might rate page one treatment in the U.S. rarely rates a single line in Pravda unless it helps convey an editorial point. Many Pravda news stories editorialize heavily to support a party position. A story on Russian black market profiteering is reported in a scolding manner. A news photograph of Washington, D.C., police beating up an anti-war demonstrator helps support an accompanying article criticizing the U.S.

But the points being made are often the real news because they show what the Soviet hierarchy is thinking. The Communist Party's ruling body, the Central Committee, appoints all key editors. Mikhail Zimjanin, the chief editor and a former ambassador to North Vietnam, is a member of the committee.

Pravda editors scoff at the idea that they are simply mouthpieces of the committee, however. "We are responsible for Pravda. We are not dictated to in our day to day operations," claims Vadim Nekrassov, the scholarly looking deputy editor. But the editors thoroughly understand the party line and are imbued with Lenin's concept that "freedom of the press is freedom for the political organizations of the bourgeoisie."

Naturally, Pravda never publishes any criticism of the Kremlin leadership. Kremlinologists believe there is little chance indeed that the paper will deviate from the Central Committee line. But if you're a Russian trying to follow the party line, this has a value of its own.

An especially valuable key to the party line is the "leader," a 900-word article printed on the left of the first page nearly every day. Conceived by Lenin himself and written in editorial style, the leader interprets or stresses some phase of current party doctrine. Diverse in subject matter, leaders may urge greater cooperation with developing countries, advocate increased industrial use of computers or criticize Western nations.

Other serious articles on domestic or international subjects fill the rest of Page 1. On most days, another five pages complete the paper. Pravda's thinness, of course, is one reason the paper can sell so cheaply and still show a profit.

Page 2 covers internal party affairs, official appointments, economic problems and letters to the editor. The third page is devoted to science, literature, the arts and culture. Page 4 stresses reports of foreign Communist and Socialist parties.

Page 5, the newsiest in the paper, carries reports from Pravda's 42 bureaus abroad, including one in Washington and another in New York. Either on its own or through the Soviet news agency, Tass, Pravda has use of most major foreign press services, including the Associated Press and United Press International.

Page 6 covers sports, travel, the theater and other leisure activities. When the Soviet hockey team wins a world championship, the whole page may be devoted to the victory. But if a Soviet team is walloped on a playing field, Pravda might not print a single line about it.

Throughout the paper are numerous official documents and statements printed verbatim. Typical is a statement by Marshal Andrei Grechko that starts: "In the conditions brought about by the aggressive policy of imperialism, Soviet soldiers must work even harder to perfect their combat skill, persistently to master the military equipment and weapons entrusted to them, tirelessly to increase their vigilance and combat readiness, to strengthen discipline and vigilantly to protect their beloved motherland."

Pravda editors explain that as an official party organ, the paper is obliged to print major documents in full. But the official statements have contributed heavily to Pravda's world-wide reputation for being a bore. This reputation irritates Pravda editors. "We don't think we're perfect," says Mr. Tsukasov, the managing editor. "But we do try to do a job for our readers and our rising circulation shows we must be doing many things right."

To help find out what readers want, Pravda a few years ago conducted a capitalist-style readership survey. The editors were pleasantly surprised to find that 70% of the readers said they read the leader article. But the survey also showed that the average reader was 40 years old, that the paper fared relatively poorly in the under-25 market and that readers in general wanted more coverage of day-to-day news events.

Since the survey, Pravda has tried to brighten its pages, and this effort has clearly boosted the paper's popularity. Says one diplomat who has been here for years: "It's nowhere near as dull as it used to be. In fact I would be lost without it."

One section that appears exceptionally popular is the unusual letters department. This part of the paper has turned into a combination national complaint bureau and idea exchange. Last year Pravda received 371,000 letters to the editor.

Pravda employs a staff of 50 to handle the flow of these letters, which currently averages 1,300 a day. About 75% of the letters involve citizen gripes or suggestions. Lenin himself advised paying particular attention to this mail, and current Soviet leaders apparently do so.

When the letters department notices a significant trend in the mail, it prepares a detailed memo on the change and sends it to the appropriate Kremlin official. Recent memos deal with the numerous complaints about inadequate sports facilities and poor fuel distribution. Prime Minister Kosygin will receive a copy of the latter. Anatoly Blatin, who heads the letters-to-the-editor department, is one of three Pravda officials who has a direct telephone line to the Kremlin.

The letters section includes five reporters who

travel the country following assignments based on incoming mail. With the help of Pravda's 62 correspondents scattered around this vast country, they check complaints and interview letter writers. No letter appears in Pravda until all the facts are double-checked. Letters often produce action. Readers who find battles with the bureaucracy frustrating know that even in the most remote places, Pravda can often get things done. From Kazakhstan, Central Asia, a Mrs. Kaidacheva recently wrote to complain that the local school lacked a gymnasium even though an empty garage nearby could be renovated for the purpose. Pravda promptly contacted the local authorities in the remote town. The garage promptly became a gym.

From Mirny, a diamond-mining community in northern Siberia, the Audeev family complained that the postal system had lost a package and that postal bureaucrats had simply shrugged their shoulders. After a Pravda reporter called, the whole local post office apparently started hunting feverishly for the package— and found it promptly.

Some letters produce Pravda stories, but not always the stories the letter writer had in mind. Mr. Blatin recalls a letter from a village near Kharkov complaining of the dire poverty of a widow with 10 children. Expecting a story denouncing cold-hearted bureaucrats who failed to handle their welfare jobs, Pravda dispatched a reporter. But the reporter found that welfare officials were caring for the family properly. So instead of damning the bureaucrats, the subsequent Pravda story condemned welfare chiselers.

Despite meticulous attention to such letters, Pravda gets by with only 300 editorial employes, including 140 writers. Considering the paper's circulation, this is an unusually small staff. But Pravda relies on outsiders for fully two-thirds of its copy.

On the staff itself, starting reporters (who have generally learned the ropes on smaller papers) earn the equivalent of $135 a month base pay. Top editors earn up to about $600 a month. A prolific reporter can also double his pay by writing extra stories for bonuses ($45 to $75 for a 900-word leader, for instance).

Among other perquisites, employes can enjoy cut-rate vacations at resorts that Pravda operates on the Black Sea. Discriminatory though it may appear, editors and reporters receive a month's vacation every year, while technicians are entitled to three weeks and printers get only two.

Printing Pravda is an awesome task. Because the Soviet Union sprawls 6,000 miles from east to west, the paper prints in 42 different locations across the nation. To service the 16 plants farthest from Moscow, Pravda photographs the pages of the next day's paper and transmits the image via cable or even satellite; printing plates are then made up at the plants. A special service of Aeroflot, the Soviet airline, delivers matrices of the paper to the other printing plants; these are used to cast metal plates from which the papers are printed.

Delivery of the printed paper to individual readers is also a problem. In some remote areas of Siberia, the daily Pravda must even be flown in by helicopter.

Yet the system works. Ivan Ponomarev, circulation manager, proudly claims: "You can get the paper the same day in all major places in the Soviet Union." With a seven-hour time difference, citizens in the Far East city of Khabarovsk may be reading their morning Pravda before some Muscovites have even gone to bed the previous night.

—RAY VICKER

1971

Time and Newsweek

NEWSWEEK marches on.

The nation's most imitative weekly shows signs of narrowing the circulation and advertising gaps between it and the world's most imitated weekly. As for any credibility gap between the magazines, Newsweek would have you believe that it is far more believable than Time. And, says Newsweek, Time is running scared.

Time scoffs. "It's like the Chicago Tribune saying it's the world's greatest newspaper," says Otto Fuerbringer, managing editor of Time, in dismissing Newsweek's claim to be the fairest and most quoted newsweekly. (The same advertising boast is made by U.S. News & World Report.) As for Newsweek's claim that it "separates fact from opinion," Mr. Fuerbringer says: "They may catch some boobs who believe that slogan. But if they did separate fact from opinion, Newsweek would be unreadable."

Some readers and advertisers—certainly not all boobs—apparently do believe the Newsweek claims. In the first six months of this year, Newsweek's newsstand sales rose 9%; Time's fell 6%. In the same period, Newsweek gained 26 pages of advertising from a year earlier; Time lost 24. But Time still leads. It has 3.7 million weekly circulation in the U.S.; Newsweek has 2 million. Time had 3,396 ad pages last year; Newsweek had 2,999.

If Newsweek does ever catch Time, it will just be

more proof that Henry R. Luce hit upon a winning formula when he started Time in 1923. For Newsweek,
which was founded in 1933 and sold to the Washington
Post Co. in 1961, is very much like Time. Several of its
top people are former Time staffers. The magazines
cover the same fields—though Time usually interprets
events with more positive authority than the less cock-
sure Newsweek.

The writing in each is polished, though Newsweek's
is less uniformly so than Time's. In a mixed metaphor
in a special Vietnam issue last week, Newsweek said:
"The excesses of the extremists are only the frosting on
the iceberg." Both magazines rely less on stylistic tricks
than they used to. But each still likes obscure words.
Time recently used paradigm, eupeptic, aphronic and
detritus; Newsweek recently used matutinal, muzzy and
smarmy.

Each likes puns. (Time: The Queen Elizabeth and
Queen Mary are "known to be sailing in financial
straits." Newsweek: "In Watts, about 13 miles from Hollywood as Jim Crow flies. . . .") People quoted in Time
don't say things; they snort, snarl, wail, declaim and
allow. Newsweek people rue, intone, quip, muse, mutter
and huff.

Each loves adjectives and descriptive phrases, and
some phrases appear to be in special favor. On May 12,
Time referred to "well-scrubbed young girls" at an event
in Europe. On May 22, Newsweek referred to "well-
scrubbed girls" at an Illinois high school. And on June
5, Newsweek referred to "well-scrubbed White House Fel-
lows." In Newsweek's May 29 issue, both comic Ron
Carey and race driver Mario Andretti are likened in ap-
pearance to altar boys.

Sometimes, though, words trip them up. Last year,
in a story about singer Nancy Ames, Newsweek noted
she was graduated from Bennett Junior College, which

it described as "tony." But the typesetter used a capital
T, so as a result Newsweek had Miss Ames graduating
from "the Tony Bennett Junior College." Time, which
often uses foreign words and phrases, got burned when
it printed a letter allegedly signed by four Indians. The
names actually were obscenities in Hindi.

But if the magazines are much alike in form and
format, they are becoming increasingly different in content. Objectivity has never been considered a virtue at
Time, and its editors say it still isn't. The magazine is
usually friendly to big business, always anti-Communist
and definitely enthusiastic about the war in Vietnam,
which some outsiders have labeled "Time's house war."
("It's the right war in the right place at the right time,"
says associate editor and chief war writer Jason Mc-
Manus.)

Newsweek maintains it is more objective, though
its news stories on the war could hardly be called dovish. But, lacking the heritage of the strong Luce viewpoint, Newsweek is freer to air opposing views. A column
on the economy is written in rotation by liberal economist Paul A. Samuelson, moderate Henry C. Wallich
and conservative Milton Friedman. Political columnists
Emmet John Hughes and Walter Lippmann are Vietnam doves, while Kenneth Crawford is a mild hawk and
Raymond Moley a strong hawk.

One example of how the two magazines played a
story differently: When physicist J. Robert Oppenhei-
mer died this year, Time reported his death in one paragraph, recalling revocation of his security clearance but
omitting that he was later honored at the White House.
Newsweek devoted two and a half columns to a respect-
ful obituary.

Newsweek likes scoops and likes to make news—
with such disclosures as the probable retirement of Justice Tom Clark, the U.S. plan to move bombers to Thai-

land and the Vietnam peace feeler Sen. Robert Kennedy brought home from a trip to Europe. But Time editors often display a heartier appetite for news that has already been reported than news that hasn't. A former Time man in Saigon claims that for fear of having good stories turned down by New York editors, he leaked them first to the New York Times. Time editors read them in the Times, he claims, and then usually sent cables ordering the Saigon bureau to get the story. "The editors are more comfortable following on a story than leading," he says.

Time generally treats avant-garde plays, movies, music and art less kindly than Newsweek. Time dismissed The Chelsea Girls, a low-budget film by Andy Warhol, as "a very dirty and a very dull peep show." Newsweek hailed the film as "one of the most powerful, outrageous, relevant and noticeable movies anyone anywhere has made for years."

Time, however, is more inclined than Newsweek to see the light side of dark events. It gathered jokes about the Middle East conflict and put them in a special, well-displayed box headed Blintzkrieg. (Sample joke: "Ralph Nader launched a campaign to provide Arab tanks with back-up lights.")

Only recently have Newsweek editors shed their inferiority complexes. They no longer discard a story idea simply because Time had it first, and they have all but stopped worrying whether a cover story will duplicate Time's. Time editors express similar aloofness toward Newsweek, though they concede Newsweek has improved editorially and graphically of late.

Osborn Elliott, Newsweek's editor, who once worked at Time, thinks Time is taking Newsweek more seriously because "important people in Washington and elsewhere who used to ignore Newsweek now read it." Just to make sure that notables do read it, Newsweek sends free copies to all Congressmen, Supreme Court Justices, top officials in the Executive branch, top corporate officers and other important people. Time sends free copies to Congressmen.

Time officials assert vigorous promotion is a major reason Newsweek is quoted often. Time's own promotion has been haphazard, but that is changing. The magazine just hired a publicist to send out news releases on each week's issue.

Time also claims that its surveys show it is the favorite of bankers, brokers, Pentagon officials, doctors, college presidents and persons listed in Who's Who in America. An independent study shows that adult readers of Time are slightly better educated and more affluent than Newsweek readers and that adults spend more time at home reading Time (65 minutes per issue) than Newsweek (53 minutes).

Time is not the favorite of everybody, though. In 1964, Fact magazine, whose own journalistic methods have been criticized, devoted 21 pages to charges of "distortions, omissions and lies" from persons Time has written about. "The inaccuracies of Time are as numerous as the sands of the Sahara," author H. Allen Smith told Fact. Said Sen. John McClellan of Arkansas: "I regard Time as prejudiced and unfair in its reporting." Producer David Merrick: "As far as I'm concerned there is not a single word of truth in Time magazine." Actor Burgess Meredith: "I have been aware of inaccuracies in Time for longer than I care to remember."

"It's pretty hard to be provocative without occasionally provoking people," says James R. Shepley, Time publisher.

To show that Time has admirers, the magazine has put out a promotional packet that includes favorable quotes from such cover subjects as Sen. Jacob Javits of

New York, Los Angeles socialite Buff Chandler and publisher Bennett Cerf.

Among those who get irritated with Time are some of its own correspondents throughout the world. Time's correspondents send in 750,000 words a week. Using these wires, newspaper clips and other sources—and their own judgment—the magazine's editors and writers turn out a 50,000-word issue, over which the correspondents have little, if any, control. The correspondents chronically complain that the long and meticulously researched reports they send to New York are distorted or even ignored in the final product.

Compensating Time and Newsweek correspondents for the frustrations of being second-guessed are salaries up to $40,000, extremely high for reporters. They also have generous expense accounts and generally agreeable working conditions.

Wages and benefits are also good in New York, but tensions are often high, and the work pace is often furious. The beginning of the week is lackadaisical, but pressure mounts toward the week's end and staffers commonly work past midnight on Thursdays and Fridays. The working conditions are pretty much the same at both magazines—and they became even more equal last fall when Time quit putting out a table of liquor for the editors toiling on Friday nights.

Senior editors, competing for space and responsibility, typically put in 55 to 60 hours a week at the office, many more reading at home and in transit. "There's a good deal of dedication around here," says Marshall Loeb, a senior editor at Time who once worked 44 straight hours on a late-breaking cover story. Editors and writers don't get overtime pay, but both magazines give four to six weeks of vacation to their New York news people.

An essential cog in the editorial machinery at each

magazine is the researcher. Most are young women. Time has 65; Newsweek has 42. Early in the week they help writers by assembling newspaper clippings and other research material; occasionally, they conduct interviews. Late in the week they check writers' stories word for word for accuracy. Researchers at Newsweek underline each word after they check it. At Time, the researchers put a black dot over every word except proper names, which rate a red dot.

Despite this painstaking checking, factual inaccuracies get by with frustrating frequency. Some errors result from cribbing from erroneous newspaper stories or from wrongly interpreting a correct newspaper account. Deadline pressures make errors more likely—as they do on daily newspapers, including this one. In rushing through a cover story on Israeli Defense Minister Moshe Dayan recently, Newsweek's researchers let stand a statement that he had lost his right eye, even though the cover photo showed him with a black patch on the left.

Neither magazine corrects an error unless a reader points it out and his letter is printed. Several readers complained that an April 28 Time story about Mexican-Americans was insulting to that minority group and riddled with inaccuracies. Among them: Time said East Los Angeles has 600,000 Mexican-Americans (the approximate total is 200,000); Time said Edward Roybal is the only Mexican-American in Congress (there are three others); Time also awarded California to John F. Kennedy in the 1960 election (Richard M. Nixon won there.)

Instead of fumbling for facts or trying to write around them, writers at the newsmagazines usually type "00" for an unknown statistic and "TO KUM" or "KOMING" for other facts. They then send researchers and correspondents scurrying to supply the missing details. According to an ex-editor's possibly apocryphal account, a newsweekly writer once wrote, "There are 00 trees in Russia"—and somehow a researcher came up with a number.

Details are used to give stories a through-the-keyhole authenticity, to entertain, to titillate or to set a scene. A recent Time story on a retiring physics professor started off: "The short (5 ft. 4 in.), white-haired professor perched on a small stool, his feet hooked in the lower rung, his hands extracting scrawled lecture notes from a manila envelope. Isidor Isaac Rabi (rhymes with Bobby) gazed stolidly up at his 30 selected students at Columbia University's tiered, 286-seat Pupin physics lecture hall."

Seemingly irrelevant details like the 286 seats in Pupin Hall, the 74 steps that Newsweek says lead to the home of the late artist Edward Hopper and the Michelob beer that Time says Johnny Carson favors help make dramatic theses credible by implying that if the magazine knows such little facts, it must know major facts, too.

But even little facts can be elusive. When President Johnson presented General William C. Westmoreland with the Distinguished Service Medal last November, Life, Time's sister publication, reported that "the general was so surprised that his eyes bugged and he gave a little jump." But Time said: "Like the good soldier he is, the general betrayed no surprise, did not even turn his head when he heard the news."

(The two Time Inc. publications also disagree on a more substantive issue. Life feels that questions left unanswered by the Warren Commission Report warrant another official investigation into the assassination of President Kennedy. Time's position is that "lacking any new evidence, there seems little valid excuse for so dramatic a development as another full-scale inquiry.")

Time sometimes even has differences with itself. Its views change as writers come and go. Not so long ago, for example, Time said, "Playwright Tennessee Williams often writes like an arrested adolescent who disarmingly imagines that he will attain stature if (as short boys are advised in Dixie) he loads enough manure in his shoes." Three months later, Time called Mr. Williams "an electrifying scenewright," "a consummate master of theatre" and "the greatest U.S. playwright since Eugene O'Neill." For monologues, said Time, "the theatre has not seen his like since the god of playwrights, William Shakespeare."

Newsweek gets around the problem of self-contradiction by signing its reviews and by-lining its analytical pieces. Time doesn't intend to follow. "It's not for us," says Mr. Fuerbringer, the managing editor, "because many people work on most stories and signing them with one man's name would be very difficult."

Jesse L. Birnbaum, one of 14 senior editors at Time, says that ending anonymity would "dilute the authority of the monolithic point of view." He adds: "The minute you use bylines, the reader has the right to ask, 'Is this the magazine or the writer speaking?' "

Both Time and Newsweek like not only to write about big shots but also to cozy up to them. Time takes leading businessmen on "news tours"—to Europe and the Soviet Union in 1963, Southeast Asia in 1965 and Eastern Europe in 1966.

Both magazines also cultivate college students with cut-rate subscriptions and campus talks by editors. Though Time has long been the students' favorite, it remains suspect with professors.

John C. Merrill, professor of journalism at the University of Missouri, concluded after a study of Time's political reporting that the magazine "editorialized in its regular 'news' columns to a great extent," using "a whole series of tricks to bias the stories and to lead the reader's thinking."

Many persons who fault Time's handling of national and international news in the front of the magazine are avid readers of the "back of the book," which covers business, cultural, scientific and other developments that receive cursory attention in most newspapers. The back of the book is better read than the front, say Time officials. Best read of all are medical and religious articles. "Is God Dead?" was an esoteric controversy until Time, a great popularizer, put it on the cover. The issue sold more newsstand copies than any other Time issue last year and provoked 3,500 letters.

But even critics concede that Time's political coverage now is more balanced than in its anti-Truman and pro-Eisenhower days. Senior editor Michael Demarest says he "personally was embarrassed" by the way Time "went way out on a limb to glorify the Eisenhower Administration." He says, "It was blatant political partisanship." Though some readers continue to think of Time as Republican, it leaned slightly to JFK in 1960 and LBJ in 1964.

Political coverage isn't the only thing that has changed at Time over the years. When Time first started, its sentence structure was so irritating to some persons that it prompted Wolcott Gibbs to write in his famous 1936 New Yorker parody: "Backward ran sentences until reeled the mind." And, "Where it all will end, knows God!" Less frequent now are these backward sentences, say Time editors. (But Newsweek wrote recently: "No, she was not a candidate for Congress, stressed Shirley Temple Black. . . .")

But though Time doesn't emphasize that style any more, many people still think of the backward sentence when they think of Time. Indeed, both magazines say they are often unfairly stereotyped. Jack Kroll, a senior editor at Newsweek, laments that "so many people still think of Newsweek as a watered-down, grey, deadly dull copy of Time." And Putney Westerfield, assistant publisher of Time, says many persons "haven't read Time in years and don't know it's changed." And then he says: "They might still hate us, but they'd enjoy us more."

—A. KENT MACDOUGALL

1967

Reader's Digest

THE Bible comes in 1,232 languages and dialects. The Reader's Digest, another evangelistic publication, comes in only 14.

And that is the only publishing-success comparison in which the Digest comes off second best. Otherwise:

No publication of any sort comes near the 27 million copies the Digest sells each month. Its U.S. circulation of 16.5 million is about 60% more than the 10.4 million that runner-up TV Guide, a weekly, averaged in 1965.

Abroad, the Digest isn't too popular in Red China, where it sells only 40 copies a month. But it is the best-read magazine in Canada, Mexico, Venezuela, Brazil, Argentina, Chile, South Africa and India.

No other periodical has a circulation of more than a million in all the world outside its native land. Digest circulation tops a million in each of four foreign countries: Canada, Germany, France and England.

All this might seem a far cry from the operation DeWitt and Lila Acheson Wallace began in a basement under a Greenwich Village speakeasy in 1922, and later moved 31 miles north to a garage and pony shed in Pleasantville, N.Y. And many things, large and small, are indeed different. Circulation is up 1,800,000% from the original 1,500, and the number of employes has grown from two to 8,200—5,600 of them abroad. Headquarters since 1939 has been in Chappaqua; nearby

Pleasantville, with its cheery ring, is only the Digest's mailing address now.

The Digest has become far more than a magazine. It's a corporation that last year rang up sales of over $300 million and profits that, though undisclosed, are estimated in the tens of millions. It derived as much 1965 revenue from selling books and phonograph records as from the magazine. Last year it acquired Funk & Wagnalls Co., the dictionary and reference book publisher, and in January it launched the Reader's Digest Almanac. This summer it will bring out the Reader's Digest Encyclopedic Dictionary. Yesterday it announced plans to purchase National Advertising Service, Inc., which sells advertising in college newspapers.

The magazine, by winning readers' loyalty to the Digest name, remains the base for all this. But it too has had some changes. It didn't accept ads until March 1955, but since has run $413.5 million worth. Last year it ran fourth among magazines in ad revenue, trailing Life, Time and Look.

As to content, some critics charge the Digest no longer merits its name. Only 41% of the articles in its U.S. edition last year were genuine digests of material from other periodicals, or from books or speeches. Another 34% were "originals" written directly for the Digest, and 25% were "plants"—pieces that the Digest plans, assigns to authors and pays for, then gets some other periodical to publish so that the Digest can "reprint" them. Last year the Digest planted articles in 40 publications, ranging from such obscure ones as Irish Farmers' Journal to such prestigious ones as the Saturday Review, Harper's and The New York Times Magazine.

Harry L. Harper, Jr., a Digest vice president and executive editor, says this "placement" system "helps preserve the reprint character of the Digest." But it has had some odd results. The Digest once ran an article 468 words longer than the magazine from which it was supposedly condensed, and The Psalms: Hymnbook of Humanity will appear in the April Digest three weeks before Christianity Today carries the "original." Authors know anything written for the Digest may be planted, but one says they often find out where only in this way: "You meet a friend and he says 'I see you're writing for The Rotarian.'"

For all the changes, though, two all-important things are still the same. DeWitt Wallace, now 76, and his wife, who own 90% of the stock, still run the show ("he is the Digest and the Digest is he" says Hobart Lewis, who succeeded him as president 15 months ago). And the Wallaces, each a minister's child, still follow an editorial formula that is strongly missionary in tone—though intellectuals often find the Digest's gospel suffocatingly bland.

The magazine cherishes articles of spiritual advice, self-help pieces and inspirational stories about people who have risen above adversity. Personal-adventure stories, with emphasis on triumph over hardship, and folksy pieces about children, teen-agers, animals and nature are regular fare, too.

Above all, the magazine accentuates the positive, minimizes the negative and strikes a note of hope whenever possible. (Sometimes its hope proves illusory. An article on How Los Angeles Eases Racial Tensions appeared in October 1964, 10 months before the fiery Negro riots there.)

"We are accused of dealing in sweetness and light," says President Lewis. "We try to look on the constructive side—there's no value in hand-wringing—and if you wrestle with a problem long enough, you usually find a solution."

Not all is bland, however. Articles about the "Communist menace" appear regularly, and so do such pieces as New Grab for Federal Power: Unemployment Benefits which appeared in the February Digest. Reo M. Christenson, professor of political science at Miami University in Ohio, has counted more than 300 Digest pieces since 1944 that he says develop the themes "that Federal officials are congenitally extravagant, that deficit spending and the national debt threaten disaster, that Federal taxes are an insupportable burden, that the Federal bureaucracy bungles and botches as it bloats, and that Federal power is a menace to the liberties of every American great and small."

An explanation from President Lewis: DeWitt Wallace "is a Scotch Presbyterian. He believes everyone ought to order his own world and do a good job."

To Mr. Lewis, this emphasis on self-reliance leads logically to Digest "opposition to big government in areas where local government or private initiative can do the job." He adds that though the Digest doesn't endorse candidates, "some of the principles of the Republican Party are closer to the Digest philosophy than Democratic Party principles."

Articles on health are important to the Digest formula, too. Like most Digest pieces, they try to strike the note of hope—to an extent that has brought the Digest angry criticism from doctors for allegedly prematurely reporting new, often experimental, drugs and treatments. The Digest, however, is proud of its record; Mr. Lewis says it "pioneered in popular medical journalism." Much of the criticism has subsided since the Digest began getting many of its medical articles printed first in such medical journals as Today's Health, an organ of the American Medical Association.

View-with-alarm is scarcely absent from the Digest's health pieces, though. The magazine began crusading against cigaret smoking in its very first issue (with a warning that "one cigaret will kill a cat") and has never let up. The April Digest will carry the magazine's 37th anti-smoking article: Story of an Ex-Smoker by Louis Fieser, a Harvard chemistry professor, member of the advisory committee to the Surgeon General that indicted smoking as a health hazard, and a four-pack-a-day man until he contracted lung cancer last year.

Digest editors, though they try to follow their magazine's advice, have found it hard to quit smoking too. James Monahan, a senior editor, puffed more than two packs a day while writing eight anti-cigaret stories; he now smokes a pipe regularly and a cigaret occasionally. DeWitt Wallace himself was a heavy cigaret smoker until he quit altogether five years ago.

Finally, but far from least important in the editorial formula, are articles on sex—treated from a viewpoint that Hobart Lewis, who is an executive editor, frankly says is "square." He adds: "We don't regard being square as a liability. We stand for some pretty fundamental values." The Case for Chastity, an article that first appeared in the Digest in 1937 and was reprinted in 1962, and What I Have Told My Son, in the forthcoming May issue, exemplify the genre.

"Sex and self-help articles are the most promotable" parts of the formula, says George F. Sprague, a Digest circulation director. This self-appraisal is reflected in the "blurb" glued to the cover of all newsstand copies of the Digest. The February blurb touted a lineup of articles that pretty well summarizes the Digest's fare: Sex and the Teen-Age Girl; Breathe Right—And Stay Well; How to Go to College on Nothing a Year; 53 Ways to Entertain Once; Science Tackles the Baldness Problem; and How to Live With a Woman.

Like all missionaries, the Wallaces have encountered unbelievers; non-"squares" of several varieties find the formula either lamentable or laughable. A current joke in publishing circles concerns the writer who produced the perfect Digest article. Originally he wrote it as a how-to-do-it piece; the Digest successively urged him to transform it into a personal-experience story and to inject notes of spiritual uplift and of concern over the menace of communism. It emerged entitled: How I Fought a Grizzly Bear for the FBI and Found God.

In a more serious intellectual vein, Ernest Dichter, president of the Institute for Motivational Research, says the Digest preaches "a childlike positivism" that is "as good as taking two Miltowns. It tries, like a good minister, to console, to get people to live harmoniously together, rather than to burn out social ills. (But) it may be harmful just because it doesn't stir people up and get them mad."

A spokesman for the National Association for the Advancement of Colored People expresses a criticism of the Digest common in the civil-rights movement: "They do have success stories about Negroes who have risen above the barriers, but not about people who fight the barriers."

Though the Digest prints frequent pieces both about corruption in unions and about labor leaders who try to fight it, "the anti-labor pieces far outweigh the pro-labor pieces, or the neutral or factual pieces," says Albert J. Zack, a spokesman for the AFL-CIO. Also, he complains, the Digest, unlike most periodicals, doesn't print corrections of factual errors or letters expressing opposing views—"there's no place to set the record straight."

Whatever critics think of their views, however, Digest editors are rated thoroughly skilled professionals by magazine competitors. The editors who condense articles for the Digest are credited with carrying on ably the tradition William Roy DeWitt Wallace began at 10

when he cut his name to DeWitt Wallace. Joe Mc-
Carthy, a free-lance writer, says the Digest's cutting job
on a series on the Ford family that he originally wrote
for Holiday "improved the piece 75% or 100% without
losing any of the flavor."

The New Yorker might disagree; since 1944 it has
refused to let the Digest reprint anything from its pages
because, it said, the Digest condensations "made hash"
of the originals. But the Digest says no other major
magazine has taken such a stand. The Digest pays eight
important magazines an undisclosed annual fee for allowing it to reprint anything they run. It pays other
magazines and newspapers $250 to $300 for each page
that reprints fill in the Digest; the author gets a like
sum.

These payments are important to small, struggling
magazines, and authors often get more than they
earned on the originals. Last year the Digest reprinted
non-planted pieces from such obscure publications as
Sodalis and Rutgers Alumni Monthly, though its favor-
ites were Time and The Saturday Evening Post (11 reprints from each).

The predictability of the Digest's formula, however
much it may make Mr. Dichter and others writhe, is
considered by competitors to be one of the most important parts of the magazine's appeal. "The reader knows
just what he'll find, and that's as comfortable as putting on an old shoe," says an executive of another magazine.

In any case, there's no questioning the Digest's
hold on its readers, who are predominantly middle-
class. In the Northern Plains and Mountain states it
reaches phenomenal proportions—perhaps because
DeWitt Wallace hails from that part of the country (he
was raised in St. Paul, studied at Macalester College
there while his father was its president, and has since

given the college $40 million). More than two of every
five households in Idaho take the Digest, and nearly two
in five in the Dakotas, Montana and Utah.

The world-wide appeal of what would seem to be
such a corn-fed American product might seem more
surprising, but it is equally undeniable. It has, at times,
provoked bitter resentment abroad. The Digest's Cara-
cas office was bombed in 1963 and the Buenos Aires office in 1964.

Nevertheless, the growth continues. The Digest's
year-old Chinese edition already has attained a circulation of 100,000, mostly in Hong Kong, Taiwan and Sin-
gapore, and there is now some thought at the Digest of
starting a Thai-language edition. Paul W. Thompson,
Digest executive vice president and general manager,
voices only one mild complaint about overseas operations: "We're running out of languages for new editions."

The Digest's foreign editions contained only material from the U.S. edition until two years ago, when
DeWitt Wallace finally gave in to persistent pleas from
the overseas editors and allowed them to run some lo-
cal-interest articles. The appeal of the overseas editions
is still based on articles that transcend national differences, such as those offering spiritual guidance—plus a
careful deletion of material from the U.S. edition that
might offend foreign readers.

Articles on birth control, a staple of the Digest's
fare at home, are cut out of editions read by the heavily
Catholic populations of France, Italy, Germany, Ire-
land, Latin America and French Canada. Civil-rights
pieces, such as the recent Why Negroes Riot, do not appear in the South African Digest, and in Finland, which
must avoid angering its powerful neighbor Russia, the
Digest omits such anti-Soviet articles as the recent
Communists Never Give Up.

(The Digest practices some self-censorship at home, too. Sex articles, however "square," are omitted from the Digest's 500,000-circulation U.S. school edition. The March school edition contained neither Unforgettable Sister Winifred, about the head of a hospital for unwed mothers, nor Filth for Profit: The Big Business of Pornography. "We didn't want the kids rushing out and looking for the publications described in the pornography piece," explains J. Chandler Hill, assistant director of the Digest's educational division.)

One thing the foreign editions contain that can't be found in any U.S. Digest is liquor advertising. All 29 foreign editions take liquor ads. But the U.S. edition bans not only ads for alcoholic beverages, but ads for quinine water and soft drinks portrayed as cocktail mixes.

Why? There is "perhaps no rational explanation," says Executive Vice President Thompson. Adds Charles D. Hepler, vice president and advertising sales director of the U.S. edition: "Our people drink and they realize that most people do, but liquor ads may offend some people."

Other Digest ad taboos, like the editorial content, appear to reflect the personal views of DeWitt Wallace. Cigaret, cigar and pipe ads not surprisingly are banned (though ads for cigaret lighters more surprisingly are permitted). Also banned are all religious ads and ads for a long list of drugs and health aids that the Digest considers of questionable taste or efficacy. The Digest is the only major magazine that won't take ads for Geritol, the product that is supposed to help people with "tired blood," according to Geritol's maker, J. B. Williams Co.

"They have a right to be out of step," says a Williams spokesman. "But it couldn't happen if the magazine wasn't a family-owned affair, because stockholders wouldn't permit them to turn away business." The 10% of the voting stock in the Digest's parent company,

Reader's Digest Association, Inc., that is not owned by the Wallaces is held by a charitable foundation they started. A small amount of nonvoting stock is in the hands of some 30 Digest executives, who must sell it back on retirement.

How long can the Digest keep all this up? As a sort of Papa and Mama business on a colossal scale, it might seem vulnerable to any loss of vigor by the Wallaces— but there is no sign of this whatever. DeWitt controls the editorial content as tightly as ever, is still alert and straight-bodied, and still greets visitors with a bone-crushing handshake.

Mrs. Wallace still suggests article ideas and picks cover illustrations. She also furnished the Digest's headquarters, personally buying paintings by Gauguin, Renoir, Matisse, Picasso and Chagall to adorn the walls. A decorator and flower arranger, both full-time staffers, work under her.

The Wallaces, moreover, seem to have imbued subordinates with the Digest's editorial formula so thoroughly that they could carry on that formula without a break. Hobart Lewis and other Digest editorial executives express views (scorn for Playboy and magazines of a similar sexual philosophy, for instance) that are indistinguishable from those they attribute to the Wallaces.

Reader loyalty appears to extend to anything that appears under the Digest's name—so that the Digest has hit several bonanzas outside the magazine. The Reader's Digest Condensed Book Club, begun in 1950, has 2.5 million American members; 90% of them are subscribers to the magazine. Some 1.5 million foreigners belong to foreign editions of the club.

The club issues four volumes a year. The typical volume contains condensations of four current novels and one non-fiction work, culled from 650 books read by a staff of 15 editors. The club pays $30,000 to more than $150,000 for world-wide rights to each book, or enough to make any author and his publisher ecstatic—particularly since a Digest condensation rarely cuts into bookstore sales of the original unabridged edition.

"The vast majority of our members don't read book reviews and don't go to bookstores," says John T. Beaudouin, a Digest vice president and book club editor. Adds an author: "A true book lover wouldn't have a Reader's Digest condensed book in the house."

The books are chosen by some of the same principles that underline the magazine's formula. Club members like action novels "with characters who are aware of moral choices and whom the readers respect," says Mr. Beaudouin; they don't care much for political, psychological or highly sophisticated novels. When explicit sex scenes occur in novels chosen for condensation, they are toned down or cut out. "We try to let the reader know what is going on without taking him into the bedroom and describing the brassiere being unhooked," says Mr. Beaudouin.

—A. KENT MACDOUGALL

1966

Free Lance Writers

RICHARD Blodgett quite his 9-to-5 job at Corporate Annual Reports Inc. last April to join the ranks of a glamorous profession: Free lance writer.

From a friend who edits The American Way, an inflight monthly published by American Airlines, Mr. Blodgett got an assignment to write an article on Hawaii's flora and fauna. But the editor needed the piece in such a hurry that Mr. Blodgett had no time to hop an American Astrojet to Honolulu. Instead he hopped the subway and researched the story in the New York Public Library. "The glamor isn't all it's cracked up to be," he says.

Two magazines ignored Mr. Blodgett's story ideas. "It's harder to get assignments than I thought it would be," he says. "You have to have contacts." And whereas he thought he could turn out two to three magazine articles a month, his actual ouput has been four in four months, for which he has been paid a total of $1,900. "It takes so long to do a good story, and you get paid so little for it, that it's a hell of away to make a living," says the dapper 29-year-old bachelor. "I'm working harder and earning less."

As Mr. Blodgett's experience suggests, economic survival among free lances is as precarious as was physical survival among their namesakes, the free lance knights of old who defended any castle for a fee. Nearly every deskbound newspaper reporter or magazine staffer (Mr.

Blodgett has been both) has thought wistfully of quitting and striking out on his own, writing this month for Harper's, next month for The New Yorker and then zipping off to Paris to do a piece for Playboy. But few actually take the plunge. And far fewer succeed.

Free lances tell a tale of woe that brings more tears than anything they grind out for the sob publications. Fees aren't rising, they say, and their best outlets are declining. "When the (Saturday Evening) Post went out last year, it put a whole lot of us in terrible trouble," asserts Richard Gehman, a prolific free lance who in one month once had an astounding 26 articles in 26 magazines, ranging from True Confessions to the Atlantic.

Their wives don't understand them, some say. They know no such benefits as paid vacations or sick leave. They have to deal with a gaggle of editors, who sometimes seem to edit by whim and often show little compassion for the struggling writer. And, like Mr. Blodgett, many assert their life is an unglamorous treadmill.

"Your mind is always on what you're working on," says Nicholas Pileggi, an accomplished writer who quit the Associated Press two years ago to be a full-time free lance. "At dinner, someone asks you to pass the sugar, and they have to say it four times. You become dull as a person, a bore to be around."

You must have a wife "who's willing to put off other gratification to see her husband become famous," adds Marvin Kitman, a former free lance who now is a columnist for Newsday on Long Island. "She has to be pioneer stock, never knowing where the next dollar is coming from."

If you're a newcomer, "you have to keep selling yourself and your ideas, and that can be pretty demoralizing after a while," says Richard Pollak, a former Newsweek staffer who took up the lance last year. Also,

he says, you must stay healthy. "I was perking along
and then last February I had to have a gall bladder
operation. It put me out of commission for almost two
months and out of pocket $900 for medical expenses not
covered by insurance."

Free lances can get in more of a rut than the one
they were in when employed, some admit. "Confessions
are limited, and we'd like to step out in the world," says
Harry Mazer, who with his wife, Norma, cranks out 50
to 60 confession magazine stories a year. Attempts to
sell TV soap opera scripts have failed, and a children's
book manuscript now is making the rounds at publishers. Says Mr. Mazer: "We haven't gotten out yet."

Still, there are satisfactions. "Guys get psychic income from writing for the Times," says an editor on the
New York Times Sunday Magazine. "After the story appears, you hear from book editors, magazine editors and
people you knew in the second grade." And the free
lance is his own boss. He doesn't have to live in the city
—or even the country. Ollie Stewart is a free lance who
supports himself in Paris by writing inspirational stories for Rosicrucian Digest and other religious magazines and by writing titillating pieces such as "Italy's
Swinging Sex Club" for U.S. men's magazines, and to
him "free lancing means freedom to write what I enjoy
writing; freedom to get up or stay in bed; to booze and
chase broads, to feel rich one month and worry about
rent the next."

There is also the satisfaction of becoming an expert. "If you do serious work, people begin to take you
seriously," says Alvin Toffler, who expanded a 1965 article on adaptation to rapid change into a just-published
book, "Future Shock." Furthermore, he says, "when you
are an expert on a subject where there are few experts,
your expertise becomes valuable." Among other things,

he is a paid consultant on the future to American Telephone & Telegraph Co.

And, of course, some free lances can hit the jackpot. Gay Talese, a former reporter for the New York Times, has earned more than $200,000 from magazine and book income for a book about his former employer. Mr. Gehman, the writer who bemoans the passing of the Saturday Evening Post, was making $100,000 a year at his peak (he owns four typewriters and sometimes had stories going in all four), but last year he made only $17,000, he says.

The 49-year-old Mr. Gehman is an old-timer in the business, and he says editors no longer clamor for his prose. In the old days, with such magazines as Collier's, the American and Woman's Home Companion—all of which collapsed in one day in 1956—it was easier to make big money writing for the big slicks.

"It's impossible to play off magazines that exist against magazines that don't exist any longer," says Julian Bach Jr., a literary agent. "And it's harder to play off a magazine that's in a profit pinch against another that's also in a profit pinch." Several new magazines have cropped up for each one that has died, but only one new entry, Playboy, is a big payer—willing to lay out $2,000 or more for an article.

These days, "a writer has to sell more articles to make the same amount of money," according to Kirk Polking, editor of Writer's Digest. Of 64 members of the Society of Magazine Writers who participated in a survey last year, only eight earned more than $30,000 a year from free lancing. Eleven made less than $10,000.

Fees range all over the lot. Nat Hentoff writes $27.50 book reviews for Commonweal and $400 record reviews for Cosmopolitan. Jazz & Pop pays him $40 for a music column, and the Village Voice gives him $50 for a weekly column on politics or the press or anything else on his mind. Playboy recently paid him $3,200 for interviewing singer Joan Baez. And the New Yorker sends him a check each week as a "draw" against the one piece a year he averages for it.

Says Mr. Hentoff: "Fortunately, I'm able to write only what I want to write." He has a business manager-accountant who, for 5%, keeps track of all the irons Mr. Hentoff has in the fire. He also has an agent, who gets 10% of Mr. Hentoff's book income.

Life magazine pays up to $5,000 for a major piece —but it's running fewer major pieces. "Considering our financial difficulties, we're happy that we haven't had to reduce what we pay our outside writers," says Tom Hyman, an associate editor. Look, which pays "top drawer" free lances $1 a word—$2,500 for a typical 2,500-word piece—has cut outside purchases and asked staff writers to take up the slack by working harder.

And writers often work weeks on a story that ends up in some editor's reject basket. The New York Times Magazine rejects a third of the pieces it assigns—and a far greater percentage of articles that come in over the transom. "They're really mercy killings," says Gerald Walker, an assistant articles editor who formerly was a free lance himself. "They're hard on the writer's vanity," he says, but not requiring the writer or a Times editor to rewrite the piece is "easier on the writer's main stock in trade—time—and on our time, too," because the piece may still end up unusable.

The Times pays $250 for the articles it assigns and kills, one third of the $750 fee for articles it runs. Many magazines pay nothing for rejected stories.

Susan Braudy says half of the two dozen pieces she has written in her two years as a free lance have been rejected, though half of the rejected pieces were subsequently sold to other magazines. The toughest turndown was a story on the women's liberation movement that Playboy assigned her. The magazine accepted the piece but wanted her to make changes to ridicule the super-militant feminists, she says. She refused, and the magazine assigned the subject to another writer. She was paid $2,000 for her efforts.

Howard H. Fogel rarely gets a rejection slip, but he's in a different league. Mr. Fogel takes pride in the quantity of his work, not the quality, spewing out 300 to 400 articles for lowpaying trade journals each year. "The better trade journals pay five cents to 10 cents a word, and $7.50 and $15 per photograph," he says. "I can do a 1,000-word story that is twice as good as a 2,000-word story, but I get only half as much for it," he says. As a result, he tends to be wordy.

Mr. Fogel's keys to survival are speed (he can write a 1,000-word story in an hour) and milking a single source for several stories. On a recent trip to Sioux City, Iowa, he visited a department store, interviewed three employes and an hour and a half later walked out with notes for stories for four publications: China, Glass & Tableware, Photo Dealer, Photo Discount Buyer and Sporting Goods Discount Buyer. Before leaving town, he also did work for National Hearing Aid Journal and Drug Topics.

For this frantic pace, Mr. Fogel says he earned $19,500 last year before travel and other expenses. He declines to disclose his net income.

Mr. Fogel supplements his income by writing puff pieces for manufacturers, which the manufacturer then places in a trade journal. The trade journal, which prints it unblinkingy, is happy because it gets a piece free. The manufacturer is happy because he gets favorable publicity. And Mr. Fogel is happy because the manufacturer pays him $100 to $150, twice his usual fee.

Most free lances have some sort of arrangements like that to provide steady income though no glory. Mr.

Blodgett, the struggling contributor to The American Way, says he couldn't make ends meet without his fees from writing a bimonthly newsletter and an annual report for his former employer. Debbie Sherwood supplements her fan magazine income (she has written 50 articles on Jacqueline Onassis without having met or talked with her) by writing liner notes for record albums and by lecturing to women's clubs on "Who Said Blondes Have More Fun?" (The 27-year-old Miss Sherwood is a redhead.)

William Furlong, a Chicago sports reporter-turned-free lance, says he made $25,000 last year from magazine writing and more than $55,000 from what he calls "invisible writing." This includes ghosting speeches and Congressional committee testimony for corporate executives and drafting and rewriting internal company reports. One Midwest company, which he won't name, paid him handsomely to investigate it thoroughly and then interview executives, asking tough questions. But he didn't have to write a word. "Fortune was going to do a story on the company, and the company wanted to go through a dry run so it would know what to expect," he explains.

Many free lances turn to authoring books, although that, too, is a difficult way to make a living. Book publishers rarely advance a writer enough money to cover his expenses during the two or three years required to research and write an important book. Mr. Talese, author of "The Kingdom and the Power," the book about the New York Times, could get no more than an $11,500 advance for that effort. To get by, he sold off various parts of the book as magazine articles, including excerpts that he sold to Harper's magazine for $10,-000.

"Willie Morris (Harper's editor) bailed me out," Mr. Talese recalls. "I didn't have next month's rent." He adds: "The trick is to try to get the most money you can for the least amount of work."

One reason getting the most money is becoming harder and harder is that some magazines' payments haven't even kept up with inflation. The Reader's Digest's minimum has less than doubled since 1940—to $2,000 from $1,200—while the cost of living has more than tripled. (But a Digest editor says that far from being too low now, the minimum was "extremely high" in 1940.)

Whether they admit it or not, even the most generous magazines are getting outside contributions at bargain basement rates. "The free lance is our cheapest source of copy," states Franc Shor, associate editor of the National Geographic. That magazine pays $2,500 to $3,500, plus expenses, for an outside article, but Mr. Shor figures a staff-written piece costs $15,000. "There isn't a good man on the staff making less than $25,000 a year, and he has a secretary and does about three pieces a year," he says.

But there are plenty of people willing to work for whatever a magazine is willing to pay. Pride in their craft, pleasure in seeing their work in print and the admiration of friends keep many free lances going.

"It's a great ego thing," says Mr. Blodgett, who vows to stick with free lancing despite his disappointing first four months. "I did a piece for New York magazine, and I heard from 15 to 20 friends who saw it. I never got that kind of response when I worked at Business Week or The Wall Street Journal."

—A. KENT MACDOUGALL

1970

Art Buchwald:

Non-Court Jester

WHEN it comes to digging up exclusives about what's going on in Washington, nobody matches Art Buchwald.

It was columnist Buchwald who recently uncovered the famous "Dawk Report" recommending elimination of the State Department by 1972 because its duties have been usurped by "the Defense Department, the CIA and Henry Kissinger." And it was the same Buchwald who recently disclosed that Vice President Agnew, despite Washington rumors, "has no intention of dumping Richard Nixon in 1972" and "even intended to give him more responsibilities than any Vice President has ever given his President before."

Mr. Buchwald, of course, works with certain advantages that ordinary journalists lack. "I never talk to anybody; facts just get in my way," he says with a puff on a big cigar. Besides, he finds it easier just to make things up.

What Art Buchwald (pronounced buckwald) does is make up funny things about serious news events, and that's not so easy. That's why he's rich and famous from writting an internationally circulated newspaper humor column that satirizes current happenings and pokes fun at the Washington Establishment. The 44-year-old columnist also is rapidly becoming a humor conglomerate—with a 12th book recently published, a new radio show and a popular lecture tour. In a new diversification move, he's writing a political satire for Broadway, called "Sheep on the Runway."

Art Buchwald the man has even more facets. He has a serious side, but he can be as funny in person as he is on paper. Sometimes he bellows like the ex-Marine that he is, but friends say he wouldn't hurt a fly, or even a politician. And the short, stocky humorist has hidden talents. "Artie," confides one friend, "is a helluva touch football player."

There were skeptics who questioned whether columnist Buchwald could make the transition to the Nixon Administration from the more flamboyant Johnson era. And it hasn't been easy. "As a humorist, I needed Lyndon Johnson—a lot more than he needed me," concedes Mr. Buchwald about his once-favorite target.

By contrast, "Writing about the Nixon Administration is about as exciting as covering the Prudential Life Insurance Co.," he says, adding hopefully: "But Spiro Agnew is coming along fast." (The Vice President has been the subject of several Buchwald columns lately, including one in which the humorist denied writing Mr. Agnew's speeches.)

Mr. Buchwald happily observes that the "Administration has livened up" recently by stirring up a controversy over TV and press news coverage. During a chance meeting at a Washington restaurant the other day, he told Herb Klein, the Administration's Communications Director: "Boy, you guys have put me back in business. Where do I send the wine?" A Buchwald column leaped into the TV news debate by chiding one network for showing the on-field violence of the recent Ohio State-

Purdue football game "rather than the peaceful scenes on the sidelines."

Buchwald-watchers maintain he has made the Johnson-to-Nixon adjustment hilariously. Some say the column hit peak form this fall with a report that the Administration was looking for an "autumn White House" in Washington as a retreat from San Clemente, Calif. The column said speculation centered on a large house at 1600 Pennsylvania Ave. but quoted a Nixon spokesman as saying, "We're looking at several houses" in that neighborhood.

Art Buchwald's column, which is syndicated by the Los Angeles Times, now appears in more than 450 newspapers—one of the largest distributions of any Washington column; as recently as 1962, the number was 85. He's believed to be among the most widely read columnists in official Washington. President Nixon, though often a Buchwald target, reads the column. And Spiro Agnew is a "Buchwald fan," although "I'm not so sure he finds the stuff about himself so uproariously funny," says a spokesman for the Vice President.

The Buchwald column appears in nearly every non-Communist country and often turns up in the Soviet Union. The Russian government sometimes reprints anti-Administration Buchwald barbs as straight news. Moscow radio, in a recent program beamed to Asia, read the Buchwald column on the "Dawk Report" as an example of a "Washington mood" demanding "that the U.S. Department of State be done away with."

(Mr. Buchwald declines to accept any rubles for the Soviet reprints. Whenever a U.S. official solemnly suggests that his columns are being used for Russian propaganda, Mr. Buchwald's horrified reply is, "Stop them.")

Part of the Buchwald attraction, some readers say, is that there often is a serious point behind his madness.

Many of his columns reflect Mr. Buchwald's own opposition to campus violence and the Vietnam war. (His
proposal for getting out of Vietnam was to create a Bay
of San Francisco incident and then bring the troops
home to protect California.) Other columns show his
concern over everyday problems like commuting or un-
solicited credit cards. "He can make a point in his 550-
word column that a serious columnist would make less
clear in twice that many words," says Rowland Evans,
co-author of the Evans-Novak Report.

Yet the humorist rarely raises real wrath because
he makes sure to be funny first and not to be
"preachy." Even the targets of his satire don't seem to
get too upset because the Buchwald humor isn't bitter
but more like good-natured spoofing. "Perhaps it's a
weakness that his satire, although effective, doesn't
really sting that much. It pricks the surface but doesn't
go to the vitals," says one prominent capital journalist.

Others argue that Mr. Buchwald's kidding, often-
whimsical approach is a strength because it commands
a wide audience for his serious insights. At any rate, the
columnist probably couldn't be more vitriolic if he tried
because "he just isn't a mean man," says a friend,
Philip Geyelin, who is editorial-page editor of the Washington Post.

Still, the Buchwald barbs often got under the skin
of former President Johnson. And some Nixon econo-
mists were peeved by a recent column in which a Buch-
wald-created economist—Professor Heinrich Apple-
baum—explained that the Administration's tax-reform
proposals would ease the burden of the wealthy while
allowing the average wage-earner only enough tax savings to buy a new tire or 200 bus tokens. "Why, it wasn't
even accurate," fumed one top-level Administration
economist.

And the columnist's fanciful views on serious topics

aren't a bit funny to some people. Irate letters are sure to pour in whenever he spoofs sex-education critics, gun ownership, the Beatles or, lately, Spiro Agnew. His office walls are lined with 20 of the best "hate" letters. Wrote one teen-aged girl: "You should be ashamed of yourself for hurting our darling Beatles. I hate you, you dirty old man."

Even Buchwald fans concede their hero's satiric barbs don't always hit the mark. Mr. Buchwald himself says he has "never been satisfied with my columns on racial issues." But by most estimates, he has a consistently high batting average.

One occupational hazard, Mr. Buchwald says, is that readers sometimes take his flights of the imagination seriously. Nothing has matched the fuss stirred up a few years ago when he wrote that FBI chief J. Edgar Hoover was "a mythical person first thought up by the Reader's Digest." Papers carrying the column were deluged with calls from readers demanding to know if the story was true. The FBI still hasn't forgiven him, Mr. Buchwald says.

"What really scares you," he says, "is when you make something up and it turns out to be true." When President Johnson sent troops to the Dominican Republic in 1965 on the ground of protecting Americans there, a Buchwald column reported that one last American, named Sydney, was being detained there so the troops wouldn't have to leave. The humorist says that when a friend at the U.S. Information Agency saw the column, he asked in all seriousness: "Who have you been talking to? That's been our problem for three weeks."

There isn't any indication that Buchwald columns directly influence government decisions. "But sometimes you incorporate them in your deliberations," says Walter Mazan, an Assistant Transportation Department Secretary. He recalls a recent meeting with air-

port managers at which officials first chuckled over a
Buchwald column on long airport walks and then seriously discussed the problem. The column had disclosed
that at Chicago's mammoth O'Hare airport, one gate-
way walk actually ended up in Davenport, Iowa.

Art Buchwald has been writing funny columns for
more than 20 years. He began newspaper work in 1948
as a $25-a-week movie reviewer on the New York Herald
Tribune's Paris edition but soon became popular for a
column called "Paris After Dark." He came to Washington in 1962, shortly after President Kennedy had canceled White House subscriptions to the Tribune which
had been critical of the Administration. Rumor had it
that the Buchwald move was in retaliation. That wasn't
true, "but I thought it best not to deny it," Mr. Buchwald says.

The humorist gets most of his column ideas from
newspaper articles, which he rips out and stuffs in his
shirt pocket. "Something just has to click," he says. A
news story about Jackie Onassis, he adds, is a surefire
trigger for his imagination; one recent column pur-
ported to interview her judo instructor.

Other ideas come from personal experience, such as
the column about long airport walks. "My transportation ones are written with real venom," he says.

On a typical working day, the humorist has already
read the Washington Post and New York Times before
leaving his northwest Washington home at about 9:15
a.m. He takes a taxi (he doesn't have a driver's license)
for the 15-minute ride to his office at 1750 Pennsylvania
Ave. about one block from the White House.

At the office, he scans the 20 to 40 letters that ar-
rive each day but soon is roaming his 13th-floor hall-
way, visiting nearby offices of the Boston Globe and
Newhouse newspapers. And the morning isn't complete
without a stop across the hall to "make trouble" for col-

umnists Rowland Evans and Robert Novak. "There's a method behind it all," he says. "In all the joshing, an idea might spark."

About 11 a.m., Mr. Buchwald sits down to write his own column. Sometimes he may have to sweat for an idea, but once he has one, the writing comes easily. "I don't stew over it," he says, and it usually takes him less than an hour to bang out a column that runs about two and a half pages of yellow typewriter paper. Although he has to write three columns a week, he hasn't any in reserve and usually works only about two columns ahead. (His Sunday column is usually written on Tuesday).

To get a quick reaction to his latest effort, Mr. Buchwald first shows it to his secretary and then takes it around to nearby offices. Mr. Evans usually gives the column a grade. ("If he gives me a B, I'll fight for a B-plus," asserts the humorist.) Occasionally, if the reception is cool, he'll do some rewriting.

(Sometimes, neighbors Evans and Novak aren't in a mood for kidding. Mr. Evans recalls one time when the two were struggling with their own column and Mr. Buchwald bounced in, waving his newest piece. Mr. Evans yelled for Mr. Buchwald to leave them alone but then broke up laughing when the elfish-looking humorist stopped, looked at Robert Novak and deadpanned, "Bob, do you realize that if something happened to Rollie, you'd make twice as much money?")

With the column wrapped up, Mr. Buchwald lunches between about 1 and 2:30 p.m. at the Sans Souci, one of Washington's better and more expensive French restaurants. He has a permanently reserved table against one wall and holds court with a bevy of friends that often include Russell Baker, humor columnist for the New York Times, columnist Mary McGrory of the Washington Star and Ethel Kennedy. He heads home from the office about 4:30 p.m. and, after dinner, often is back at the typewriter with some work—lately, polishing his play. "I feel guilty when I'm not in front of the machine," he says.

The cornerstone of Mr. Buchwald's growing empire is his column, which he repackages for about every available market. Most of his books are collections of past columns and generally sell about 35,000 hardback copies each. A radio show, begun last January, also makes use of dialogue taken from the columns. The five-minute show is broadcast five times a week on 130 educational stations and is just being picked up by 60 FM stations in several major cities.

The columns also are the core of a 45-minute "lecture" that he delivers to college students, conventions, business groups and other organizations. Among current lecturers, "probably no one is in greater demand," even though his fee of $2,500 plus expenses is about the highest around, says a spokesman for W. Colston Leigh Inc., his lecture bureau. He gives four lectures a month, nine months a year.

Mr. Buchwald gives basically the same lecture each time, although topical material is updated periodically. The speech is called "The CIA for Fun and Profit." Its topics range from Mr. Buchwald's capital graffiti— "Judge Haynsworth, call your broker"—to his theories on handling campus-building take-overs—"Instead of trying to get them out, we should brick them in." It also includes recollections of how young Art Buchwald dropped out of the University of Southern California to go to France because he heard that "in Paris, the streets are lined with beds."

Part of lecturer Buchwald's attraction is the engaging way he looks and talks. He looks humorous, like a roundish pixie. He wears hornrimmed glasses, and a large cigar usually protrudes from one side of his mouth. (He smokes six to eight cigars a day.) And his remarks are delivered with a mock seriousness or indignation that makes it sound as though he really believes what he's saying.

Lately, much of his time has been taken up writing —and rewriting—his first Broadway play, which is scheduled to open Jan. 19. The play is about a political-appointee ambassador in a small country in the Himalaya Mountains. One day a hawkish columnist named Joe Mayflower arrives, "and all hell breaks loose," Mr. Buchwald relates.

Mr. Buchwald denies that the columnist in his play represents Joseph Alsop, the real-life pundit. But columnist Stewart Alsop—Joe's less hawkish brother— isn't so sure. "Why," he asks, "does everybody call me Stewart Mayflower?"

Not everything Art Buchwald does is successful. A few years ago he collaborated with the Times' Russell Baker on a movie outline that didn't sell. According to this script, Nikita Khrushchev's nephew came to the U.S. and joined the John Birch Society. But movie producers said it was "too implausible," Mr. Baker says, adding caustically that not long afterward Joseph Stalin's daughter came to the U.S. "and joined the Book-of-the-Month Club."

Nevertheless, Mr. Buchwald has come a long way for a Long Island boy who was raised in foster homes and dropped out of high school to join the Marines during World War II. His annual income now totals about $200,000. And he turns down other income opportunities by refusing to do product endorsements or commercials.

In real life, friends say, the humorist is a friendly, sensitive man. "He can be blustery and loud, too," says Elaine Marcisso, his secretary for the past six years. "But he's the kindest man I've ever met," she says. Others say that he freely gives time and money to charities and hospitals, especially those involved with children.

What many children know is that Art Buchwald is a mythical person who is really the Easter Bunny. A couple of hundred kids and their parents gather each year at the Buchwald home for a traditional party at which the chunky humorist, according to one participant, dresses up in "a flea-bitten rabbit suit and runs around like a Pied Piper." The kids have only a few doubts. Columnist Robert Novak recalls that at this year's party, his three-and-a-half-year-old daughter wanted to know, "Daddy, why is the Easter Bunny smoking a cigar?"

"What people don't understand about Buchwald," says Mr. Novak, "is that he isn't just a funny man. He cares deeply about things." And he does work hard to keep informed on current topics. But he also likes to joke with friends and frequently tries out column ideas in conversations. He often sends friends funny telegrams—collect.

—RONALD G. SHAFER

1969

Clive Barnes:
Man on the Aisle

CLIVE Barnes confesses he's lazy. As dance and drama critic of the New York Times, Mr. Barnes only goes to the theater about 10 times a week, writes six or seven daily reviews and a lengthy Sunday article, re-reviews long runs and shows with cast changes, contributes regularly to magazines and irregularly to several books he's writing—and lectures twice a week at New York University. He sleeps daily, however, usually from about 2 a.m. to 7:30 a.m.

Mr. Barnes, a London export to Broadway, with British self-deprecation shrugs off labors other newspapermen regard as prodigious. He says he is a journalist, someone "too idle to get a proper job."

Many theater people see Mr. Barnes as more than a journalist. Simply because he is the daily drama critic of the New York Times, they cast him as The Most Powerful Man on Broadway. Obviously, some plays fail though the Times critic likes them and others succeed despite his panning them. Yet "without the endorsement of the Times," says Managing Editor Clifton Daniel, "a play would find it much harder to succeed on Broadway." Adds Mr. Daniel: "The Times critic, what-

97

ever his name, is the most influential critic in New York."

Mr. Barnes consciously tries to undermine this supposed power. He writes in a light, chatty, first-person style to let readers know they're getting one man's opinion of a play, not necessarily the final word. (In one of his dance reviews of a "children's ballet," for instance, Mr. Barnes showed he was a parent as much as a critic by revealing that his daughter vomited on the way home in the taxi.)

Nevertheless, the Barnes impact is startling—and his frequently is the final word. Shows he doesn't like tend to flop. On the other hand, a clearly doomed production that had posted its closing notice underwent a financial revival this spring after Mr. Barnes urged readers to see it.

Whether any Times drama critic has more power to fold plays than breathe life into them is a continual subject of controversy. But there's wide agreement that the 1967-68 season, which coincided with Mr. Barnes' first year as drama critic, was one of the best in recent years, both artistically and financially. Variety, the entertainment industry newspaper, reported that new box office records were set by a gross of $58.9 million for an aggregate of 1,257 playing weeks.

Some say Mr. Barnes helped a lot. Producers hail his overall enthusiasm for theater and particularly his receptivity to theatrical innovation. His two favorable reviews of Hair, the hippie musical that outraged many in the over-30 generation, are credited with propelling the show from Off-Broadway into a Broadway smash.

Mr. Barnes, who is 41, and currently wears modish muttonchops, said Hair was the first "musical in some time to have the authentic voice of today rather than the day before yesterday" but acknowledged that he couldn't repeat some of the lines in a family newspaper.

(But his review, even without the dirty words, was quite readable. Wrote he: "At one point—in what is later affectionately referred to as 'the nude scene'—a number of men and women (I should have counted) are seen totally nude and full, as it were, face.")

Theater people on Broadway, Off-Broadway and Off-Off-Broadway are impressed by the energetic reviewer. Comments about him sometimes read like rave notices:

"The best critic the Times has had, and a very affirmative force in the theater."—Producer Theodore Mann.

"The hardest-working drama critic. His enthusiasm has shown up all the other critics."—A veteran Broadway press agent.

"A very good dance critic and a pretty good drama critic and an excellent journalist. He writes at length about plays and doesn't need a week to do it."—Playwright Sidney Kingsley.

Mr. Mann says that Mr. Barnes is a "very constructive" critic who is creating a climate especially conducive for new writers. Others say Mr. Barnes is writing reviews that will lure interested, "live" audiences back from movie houses into legitimate theaters.

Mr. Barnes loves the theater and, fortunately for himself, finds that he can "almost enjoy seeing a bad play more than a good one." When a play is bad, he says, "There's always something to watch—a good actor, an interesting stage bit." In any event, he never walks out; there's the danger of missing some worthwhile business in the last act or of providing a gossip columnist with material for mischief.

When Mr. Barnes doesn't like a play, he lets his readers know. His one-word review for the London Daily Express of a production called The Cupboard: "Bare." But the Times critic claims that neither he nor any other critic can kill a good play with a bad notice. "No producer has ever been able to tell me of a good play that was killed by the critics," he claims. He says producers use critics as scapegoats, and he says he isn't surprised that so many shows close as failures. "I'm just surprised they open," he says.

Of 56 shows that opened on Broadway last year, 26 ran less than a month; a dozen of these lasted a week or less. Mr. Barnes holds that "a third or more" of Broadway shows open though they have no chance of success and that this is "obvious to everyone—actors, electricians, even the producer." Productions that are practically vanity shows for authors are nevertheless bravely staged, he says.

"A producer has to produce," observes Mr. Barnes. "He has office expenses and a name that must be kept alive. It's better for him to do a flop than to do nothing."

This season's Broadway opening shows how Mr. Barnes spends a working evening. At 7:25 he and his wife, Patricia, grab a cab at the intersection of West End Ave. and 72nd St.—they live a block away at Riverside Drive. Riding down to the Brooks Atkinson Theater (named after his most illustrious predecessor on the Times), Mr. Barnes explains there's a need to hurry but the situation isn't desperate:

While the ticket lists curtain-time as 7:15 (review nights traditionally start early to give reviewers time to write), Mr. Barnes says he's been assured the show really won't start till 7:30. "Oh, Clive," says his wife in exasperation, noting it's now 7:30.

(Last season, in a celebrated incident that illustrates the power of the Times, producer David Merrick held an opening-night curtain for 30 minutes, while other critics in their seats fumed, because Mr. Barnes was late. Mr. Barnes still missed the first 10 minutes, and in his review apologized that the plane carrying him from a Pittsburgh lecture was late. Annoyed colleagues said that Walter Kerr, whom Mr. Barnes succeeded as daily critic, was in the audience in his new capacity of Times Sunday drama reviewer and could have written the daily review.)

A few minutes after 7:30, Mr. Barnes hurries to his fifth-row aisle seat. "Well, where were you this time?" wryly asks Jack Kroll, Newsweek's critic. The curtain is traditionally late, however; Mr. Barnes has plenty of time to nod to acquaintances and to chat with a Times vice president, Turner Catledge, seated in front of him.

The season opener is called Lovers and Other Strangers, a four-playlet comedy about the war, or wars, between the sexes. Mr. Barnes, who seems mildly amused and laughs aloud (not uncontrollably) during the play, scribbles some notes in the darkened theater, somewhat unusual for him. "I felt like such a dolt when I saw other critics taking notes at plays," he says, "that I began taking them, too."

He remains seated at intermission. He stopped smoking four years ago and prefers avoiding those strangers who wouldn't hesitate to interrupt conversation or private musing to ask his opinion of a play. "Very often, I don't know what I think of a play until I get back to the office and start to write," he says.

When the final curtain falls, Mr. Barnes bolts out of his seat and, surrounded by applause for the play, strides up the empty aisle. His exit is slowed, however, by a tall, bearded man who falls in step at the theater's rear, drapes an arm around Mr. Barnes' shoulder, and asks how the critic's summer went. "Fine, fine," says Mr. Barnes, gently disengaging himself and slipping outside—and probably thwarting an inquiry about the play.

Mr. Barnes pauses outside the theater, on 47th St.

"Which way shall we walk?" he asks. "I never can decide what's shortest." He chooses the quickest route to the Times, however, along Broadway. Despite the approaching deadline, he appears relaxed: He points out a new movie theater to his wife, mentions he attended a Broadway matinee that afternoon and relates a couple of anecdotes involving a former Herald Tribune critic named Howard Barnes. Using a key, he enters the Times through a locked rear door on 44th St., just steps from Sardi's restaurant, the after-theater spot favored by celebrities, gaping tourists and Times men other than Clive Barnes, who has never been inside.

At 9:32, early for an opening night and 1 hour and 58 minutes before deadline, Mr. Barnes walks into the third-floor editorial offices of the Times. Taking his tie off, he leafs through the coming Sunday Times drama section. This week it contains a piece by Walter Kerr that rather gently chides David Merrick for a magazine article in which the producer blasted Mr. Barnes as an incompetent play-destroyer. Mr. Barnes chats with colleagues for about 10 minutes, then finally sits down at his typewriter and starts writing.

Mr. Barnes mumbles to himself a little as he types. "At least I think it's me talking," he says. "I don't think I'm Joan of Arc." When he's almost done, a copy editor telephones to question his use of the word "butch" to describe a mannish female in the play. "Butch is the opposite of, uh, effeminate," explains Mr. Barnes. At 11, summoning a copyboy for his fifth and last page, Mr. Barnes inserts another piece of paper in his machine and writes a one-minute capsule review that he records for WQXR, the Times' radio station. On this occasion, it takes him 1 minute 11 seconds to record the review. "You're slipping," heckles an engineer.

Hurrying from the studio to the composing room, Mr. Barnes examines the proofs of his review. "How about that," he mutters, "no byline." He writes in his name, makes some typographical corrections, and debates with himself for 15 seconds whether to insert the qualifying word, quite, in front of a phrase describing the comedy as "a lot of fun." He decides against it—a decision that might net the show thousands of dollars in additional box office receipts.

Mr. Barnes, noticing that another phrase has been changed by the copydesk from "sex and the single apartment" to "love and the single apartment," rushes to discuss the change with copy editors. He is assured that this isn't a question of censorship—and he re-inserts sex for love. (In the morning paper, however, the word love mysteriously has replaced sex again.) At 11:45, Mr. and Mrs. Barnes leave the Times and catch a taxi home.

Meanwhile, at a second-floor private party in Sardi's, tension has been mounting for the cast and production staff of Lovers and Other Strangers. The traditional wait-for-the-notices gathering has thinned considerably since the free bar shut down at 11. Others straggled out after the first notices—extremely unfavorable—were delivered by the television critics. "No one wants to stick around a loser," comments a theatrical lawyer.

"But at 12:05, the party's mood picks up. "We did it, we did it, we did it," screams Renee Taylor, the play's co-author and one of the performers. "We got a rave from Clive Barnes."

The Times won't be available for another half-hour. But to quiet theatrical nerves, Broadway press agents for years have slipped money to a Times composing room man to read them the drama review as soon as it's set in type. This sneak preview has produced Miss Taylor's glee. By 12:30, the show's producer, Stephanie Sills, has obtained the paper and reads aloud the Barnes review. There is a smattering of applause at key phrases but it's soon apparent that this isn't a "money review" —a notice that results in a long line at the box office.

In retrospect, Miss Sills is grateful for the Barnes notice. The show cost $130,000 to bring to Broadway and must gross $25,000 a week to break even. At the moment, it's running barely in the red. "It could still go either way," says Miss Sills, "but without Barnes I would have closed in a few days." The Times notice was a "rave with qualifications," says Miss Sills; he stopped short of advising readers to run to see it. She blames the box office anemia on television, where two critics "clobbered" the show.

Assessing the Times' influence when a show receives mixed notices isn't difficult. Some producers think the Times' daily critic's power equals that of all the other critical voices combined, including that of the Times Sunday man, (Mr. Kerr voted against Lovers and Other Strangers, one of about 10 times he and Mr. Barnes have differed substantially in the past year.)

Mr. Kerr, who was the critic for the Herald Tribune before joining the Times, says that the Times' power is "nowhere near as absolute as people think" but that it has increased as the major New York general-interest dailies decreased from seven to three. Mr. Kerr defines the critic's function as basically affirmative. "The audience isn't dying to go to the theater," he says. "If it finds an excuse not to go, it's happy—it needs to be pushed."

Theater people say the Times daily critic can provide the biggest push. One example cited often is an Off-Broadway production this spring of two plays called Red Cross and Muzeeka. Although the plays were well-received by a Times second-stringer—Mr. Barnes was occupied elsewhere—the production was limping at the box office and ready to close. Then Mr. Barnes praised it in a piece discussing the Off-Broadway season. Says Dorothy Olim, the show's general manager: "We went from $2,200 to $5,300 in one week."

The problem of choosing between two openings is a serious one—and compounded in Mr. Barnes' case because he is a dance critic as well. Not only is Mr. Barnes likely to go to a ballet if it seems more important than a Broadway opening, but he's just as likely to prefer an Off-Broadway opening. Some conflicts are resolved by attending preview performances.

Speed helps Mr. Barnes a bit in his dual critical capacity. Once last season Mr. Barnes left a theater opening at 9:15, dashed to a later performance of a ballet—and banged out two 800-word reviews in the time most reviewers write one.

Mr. Barnes sometimes gets scripts in advance, and he tries to prepare for performances by reading the scripts or digging into background material. But his style is anything but solemn. In fact, he's criticized by some for being too-facile or glib—a fault he acknowledges may have some validity. "The difficulty is you're not writing deathless prose," he says. "You've got to engage people and generate excitement—or forget it. Newspaper reviews are still something to wrap up fish-and-chips the next day."

—FELIX KESSLER

1968

Wire Services:

AP and UPI

MERRIMAN Smith is the White House correspondent for United Press International. He rides in Presidential motorcades. He says "Thank you, Mr. President" to end press conferences. To beat the competition on a Presidential trip to the Philippines he once dictated a story via walkie-talkie while perched in a tree. His byline appears in newspapers the world over. "I have a front-row seat at history," he says.

Gary Drewes is the bureau manager of the one-man UPI bureau at Pierre, S.D. He seldom gets far from his one-room office. He does much of his work by phone. Even if a plane crashes in his territory, he covers it by phone. The only paper his work regularly appears in is the Deadwood-Lead Pioneer-Times & Call. One of his daily chores is to phone in for the water level and discharge at five local reservoirs. "I'm getting sick of reservoirs," he says.

That's the way the wire services operate. They cover the globe, telling the world of war and peace and fishermen of reservoir levels. The two major U.S. services—United Press International and the Associated Press—provide Americans with 75% of the state, national and international news they read in papers and listen to on radio and television. They fight each other fiercely for front-page space and air time.

The reporters work under pressure, and they make a lot of mistakes. (Last fall, for instance, the AP incorrectly began a dispatch: "France was forced into devaluation of its franc Friday . . .") They have clients of all political leanings, and they try to be as neutral and fair —some say bland—as possible. They are chronically understaffed, especially UPI, so few reporters have time to think about and interpret the events they cover.

Yet, says Gordon Pates, managing editor of the San Francisco Chronicle, "both services do pretty well under trying circumstances."

The wire services have the power to shrink an event into insignificance or blow it up into fame or infamy. Twice daily each service prepares a list of stories, called the news budget, which most newspapers and broadcasters—especially outside the biggest cities—rely on in evaluating the day's news. In following the budget's judgments and giving the biggest headline to the top budget story, a newspaper editor has the comforting knowledge that he's in step with hundreds of other editors.

The services are so vital to a newspaper that only a handful of the nation's 1,754 dailies try to get along without at least one of the wire services. More than 500 papers take some services from both AP and UPI.

But for all their success and their power, the wire services have their problems. Their cost of news gathering is rising in these times of frequent crises and far-flung wars. The two services spend more than $1.3 million a year reporting on the war in Vietnam, where four of their photographers have been killed and 19 other staffers wounded. Yet the number of big-city papers, the major source of revenue for AP and UPI, is steadily declining. And the competition between the two services is so cutthroat that they have trouble raising their rates, though UPI has just raised its by 10% and AP plans an 11% rise next month.

"I don't know of two outfits more destructively devoted to the American principle of free-enterprise competition than AP and UPI," says Louis Cassels, a top UPI reporter with the title of senior editor. "Competition in news gathering drives expenses up, and competition in selling drives income down."

The result is a cost squeeze that causes the services periodically to "downhold" expenses, as wire service men say in the parlance of their trade, by not filling vacancies and cutting corners in other ways. Despite the downhold, the AP, a cooperative owned by its newspaper members, increasingly has trouble breaking even. And UPI, 95% owned by E. W. Scripps Co. and 5% by Hearst Corp., has lost money every year since 1962. Lately there have been recurring rumors that UPI is for sale. Mims Thomason, UPI president and general manager, says the wire service recently received "fantastic" offers from two companies he won't name. But one rumored suitor says UPI approached it and was rebuffed.

The Associated Press spent $57 million last year, about $7 million more than UPI spent. AP has 3,100 full-time employes, more than half of them newsmen, and UPI has 2,400, most of them newsmen. The services claim that these reporters turn out 7.5 million words a day. This figure is open to dispute, however, because it includes separate counts for each story each time it goes out. Major stories go out on a dozen or so different state, national and international wires.

But however many words they produce, the wire service newsmen work hard and fast. As soon as Merriman Smith says "Thank you, Mr. President" he has to dash to a phone and dictate a comprehensive, lucid report on the wide-ranging press conference. It is, he says, "a nerve-wracking chore."

Mr. Smith's constant aim is to do a story better and faster than Frank Cormier, the AP White House correspondent, or whoever else is on the scene for AP. Sometimes it's more than a battle of words. In 1963, when President Kennedy was assassinated, Mr. Smith and the AP's Jack Bell were in the motorcade. At the sound of shots, Mr. Smith grabbed the car's radiophone and dictated a bulletin. Then, in the best wire service tradition, he ducked under the dashboard and kept the phone from a frantic and furious Mr. Bell. There are stories that Mr. Smith emerged bruised and battered by Mr. Bell, but Mr. Smith now denies this. Mr. Smith won a Pulitzer Prize for his coverage of the assassination.

UPI didn't look quite so good on the next Presidential trip to Dallas, on Feb. 27, 1968. That time, the UPI story—not by Mr. Smith—began:

DALLAS (UPI) — President Johnson made a sudden, swift trip to Dallas today, his first since the assassination of President John F. Kennedy on Nov. 22, 1963. He rode in a motorcade past the Schoolbook Depository Building from where Kennedy was shot to death and commented:

"It's good to be back."

The statement, actually made earlier on Mr. Johnson's arrival at the airport, caused gasps when it came over UPI tickers in newsrooms around the world. UPI rushed out a substitute lead eliminating the "unfortunate juxtaposition."

UPI has a reputation among critics in some newsrooms for inaccuracy and overexuberance. Its biggest goof occurred in 1918 when United Press, a predecessor of United Press International, reported the signing of the Armistice four days early. "We're still living down the premature Armistice," complains H. Roger Tatarian, UPI's vice president and editor. Indeed, some newspaper editors still are reluctant to run a UPI scoop until they see it confirmed on AP.

AP, conversely, got tabbed long ago with being dependable but stodgy. But some newspapermen say that this reputation is no more deserved than is UPI's. "Both services have tried to correct their weaknesses," says Mr. Pates of the San Francisco Chronicle.

Many editors quickly excuse stodginess and mistakes of fact from both services. They know reporting and writing under fire are difficult. And many newspaper managements have a reputation as pennypinchers that will put up with almost anything as long as it is inexpensive. "Most small papers don't seem to give a damn about the quality of wire service copy—as long as the price is kept low and they can get it delivered on tapes" from which type is set automatically, says Norman E. Isaacs, executive editor of the Louisville Courier-Journal and the Louisville Times.

The Louisville dailies, which Mr. Isaacs numbers among the 20 or so U.S. papers that aspire to be great and care what they print, used to take both AP and UPI, but they dropped UPI last June. "We decided to invest the savings in five or six top investigative reporters," says Mr. Isaacs. What's more, he says, the Louisville papers now take so many supplemental services that they no longer need both AP and UPI.

The supplemental services, which stress interpretation, analysis and background, are an increasing headache for the already troubled wire services. The three leading supplementals—operated by the New York Times, the Los Angeles Times jointly with the Washington Post, and the Chicago Daily News jointly with the Chicago Sun-Times—have 400 newspaper clients in the U.S. and 200 overseas.

The Beacon Journal, in Akron, Ohio, gets all three

supplementals along with the AP wires, and executive editor and publisher Ben Maidenburg says he prefers "if at all possible" to publish no AP stories on the paper's front page. He says that the supplemental services, besides being more analytical go only to him and not to radio and TV stations in the area. "Why should I put out a newspaper that I can hear on radio and TV?" he asks.

Mr. Maidenburg says, however, that he is not dissatisfied with the Associated Press. "AP covers the news in a hell of a hurry, and this is what we expect of it," he says.

The wire services are short on interpretation and analysis for several reasons. Mainly, their people rarely have the time to sit around and think. But also, some editors quietly acknowledge that clients are offended by some interpretive stories. "We can't crusade because we have papers of every complexion under the sun," says Wes Gallagher, general manager of the Associated Press. "A crusade that pleases one is anathema to another."

Anathema to an influential Texas daily was a 2,000-word AP story on the drive of Mexican-Americans for better working and living conditions in the Southwest. AP sent out the story in August 1967, for use two weeks later. The Texas daily protested that the story was alarmist in reporting that Mexican-Americans might riot. AP agreed the article was alarmist and killed it. "AP quivered and trembled and killed a pretty important story," says Dave Smith, the author. Feeling "unfairly censored," he quit.

Even when AP does sanction an interpretive piece many papers don't use it. "Small and medium-sized papers are so busy carrying bits on running stories" that they don't give proper attention and space to the "whale of a lot of good background and interpretative stories" that AP provides, claims Kenneth MacDonald, editor and publisher of the Des Moines Register and Tribune and a former director of the AP.

If AP and UPI don't go overboard on analysis, though, they do give their clients plenty of facts. While the UPI's Mr. Drewes in Pierre is checking the reservoir levels, one of the five men in the AP bureau in Jackson, Miss., is reporting on the local egg market. ("Prices of large and extra-large ranged one to four cents higher, while mediums advanced one to three cents. . . .") Frank Wetzel, the AP bureau chief in Portland, Ore., has to make sure the local livestock and grain reports get on the wire every day, and David Bradley, the UPI bureau chief in Portland, Maine, has to put out weather forecasts at 6:30 and 11:30 every morning.

For this work, which sometimes borders on drudgery, the wire service men are paid well, by newspaper standards. Except in the biggest cities, the wire service men usually earn more than the local newspapermen who cover the same stories. Merriman Smith, now 55 years old, is said to earn more than $500 a week. Gary Drewes, who turned 24 last month, makes $191 a week.

Most wire service reporters work a 40-hour week, in theory. But Alton Blakeslee, an AP science writer, often works 12 to 14 hours a day at a convention. "Frequently, I don't get a chance to eat," he says. John Griffin, the UPI's executive sports editor, says he toiled for 30 consecutive days last fall during the World Series and Winter Olympics. "I lost 17 pounds," he recalls.

Besides irregular hours, AP and UPI newsmen contend with cramped quarters, battered typewriters, inadequate or nonexistent background files and the constant clatter of tickers. The nerve-jarring noise has actually caused partial loss of hearing, the newsmen's union, the Wire Service Guild, claims.

Most of AP's 108 U.S. bureaus and many of UPI's

100 are located in newspaper offices, where the wire service men work with and near the local reporters. In Lubbock, Texas, UPI correspondent Mike Wester sits amid the Avalanche-Journal reporters. "When they get something hot they give it to me right away, and I start working fast," he says.

In addition to hot tips, host newspapers often provide carbon copies of their stories. In return, wire service reporters often share reporting tasks on major stories with the local reporters. Says the AP's Mr. Wetzel in Oregon: "They use us, and we use them."

AP's big bureaus in New York and Washington originate nearly all the stories they turn out, but Samuel G. Blackman, AP's general news editor, estimates the other bureaus pick up fully 50% of their copy from newspapers. UPI's Gary Drewes in Pierre reads three dailies and 20 weeklies and monitors a radio station that is served by the opposition "to get an idea what AP is putting out" hour by hour.

It would be much simpler for Mr. Drewes to walk down the corridor in the Capitol to the AP bureau to find out what AP is putting out but that is considered bad form. It isn't bad form to plant a spy, though, and for years United Press kept a man at the New York World-Telegram & Sun (which was owned by UPI's main owner) with the primary duty of watching the AP machines. Other wire service people watch the competition through less-formal newsroom arrangements in other cities.

AP and UPI check newspapers taking both services to see whose stories are getting used. They compile tallies and publish them weekly. UPI usually fares best in the UPI tally. AP usually does best in the AP log.

Papers generally use the service reporting the highest casualties in an earthquake or other disaster. "Editors tend to go for the most dramatic. By and large they want to see the worst," says John N. Fallon, UPI foreign editor. This leads to some sniping between AP and UPI editors, with each side claiming the other tends to inflate casualty figures in order to get its story in the paper. Each service denies this, of course.

If there's one thing editors like more than blood and gore, it is speed. Thus, many papers use the first story in, whether AP or UPI. Wire service sports reporters often write their story before the game is over, just calling in an insert with the final score. A last-minute touchdown can ruin everything, however. "Sometimes you have to tear up two or three leads, says Mr. Griffin of UPI.

When newsmen aren't trying to bat out a story, they're often trying to drum up some business. Some bureau chiefs for both AP and UPI are responsible for selling the service to papers and broadcasters in their areas. "My toughest job is convincing an editor that he ought to pay more for AP than UPI," says Frank Wetzel, the AP chief in Portland, Ore. And Noland Norgaard, AP bureau chief in Denver, grumbles that many clients are "influenced more by price than quality."

The rates vary widely. A few small newspapers with a single ticker running only eight hours a day pay AP less than $30 a week. Some big-city dailies with eight or 10 wires pay well over $5,000 a week. UPI rates for big papers are generally lower than AP's. In broadcasting, the situation is reversed; UPI rates are generally a bit higher, running from $50 a week to more than $1,500.

Broadcasting is an important area for the wire services, as more Americans turn to the radio and TV as their prime sources of news and as more big-city papers go out of business. Today the competition among the wire services for radio and TV clients "is more cutthroat than ever," according to Mims Thomason, the

UPI president. He accuses AP of "really vicious rate-cutting."

Harry T. Montgomery, AP deputy general manager, disdains to reply. "I don't like to talk about them (UPI)," he says.

Small-station newscasters who "rip and read" wire service copy often seem unimpressed with whatever edge of superiority a service attains. "I don't think there's 10 cents worth of difference between AP and UPI," says James N. Rodio, general manager of station WNJH in Hammonton, N.J. Wire service editors say that unlike newspapers, which identify wire-service stories with the AP or UPI logotypes, broadcasters rarely mention AP or UPI except to blame them for an erroneous story.

"When it's right, it's theirs. When it's wrong, it's ours," says Mr. Tatarian of UPI.

AP and UPI give the stations quite a few opportunities to call attention to their errors. In 1966, radio and TV stations across the nation interrupted their programs to announce the death of James Meredith, as reported by the Associated Press.

When Mr. Meredith, the Negro who desegregated the University of Mississippi, started his civil rights walk from Memphis, Tenn., to Jackson, Miss., AP sent along a reporter and photographer. But the reporter turned back at the Mississippi line. "I figured the photographer, plus AP members in Mississippi, would protect us the rest of the way," says Samuel Blackman, the AP general news editor. "It was a mistake."

When Mr. Meredith was ambushed, Jack Thornell, the photographer, got a Pulitzer Prize-winning photo of him lying on the highway. Then he phoned in an accurate bulletin.

Also on the scene was a reporter for the Memphis Commercial Appeal. When he phoned his paper that

Mr. Meredith had been "shot in the head," an AP news-man listening to the call in the Commercial Appeal newsroom thought the reporter said "shot dead." He rushed out a bulletin on the "death."

In addition, in 1961, when UN Secretary-General Dag Hammarskjold flew to Katanga in the Congo, an AP newsman there saw a plane land. He filed a story that Mr. Hammarskjold had arrived. Only later did he learn that the UN official was dead in the wreckage of his plane miles away.

Both services have made premature election calls. UPI gave California to John Kennedy instead of Richard Nixon in 1960. In 1968, both services put Maryland in the Nixon column instead of Hubert Humphrey's.

If papers aren't always happy with wire service reporting neither are wire service reporters happy with some newspaper practices. One frustration is that newspapers usually carry local AP and UPI stories without bylines. "I very rarely see my own byline," says the UPI's Louis Cassals, who works out of Washington. "My family and neighbors really wonder what I do. I get kind of tired explaining that I'm in hundreds of papers around the world."

Most wire-service people never get a byline. These people are the thousands of stringers—part-time correspondents—who fill the services in on doings in such out-of-the-way places as Custer, S.D., and Houston, Miss. Most stringers are newsmen, but the Custer stringer, who regularly calls in forest fires, is a house-wife. And the Houston stringer, who never misses a prominent death in Chickasaw County, is a woman undertaker.

The stringers don't get rich at their part-time jobs. Rarely do they get more than $5 for an item, and several bureau chiefs say they seldom pay any one stringer more than $35 a month.

In remote areas, where stringers are scarce, some work for both AP and UPI. Neither service is very happy about this, each believing that these stringers tend to call the opposition first. Nor are they happy about leaving coverage of many college sports events to publicity directors and team managers. The editors don't worry too much about one-sided sports reports, however. "You can't do too much proselytizing in three paragraphs," says UPI sports editor Griffin.

Slanting is a real danger in coverage of racial strife, however. "Stringers try to minimize things like that because it hurts the local economy," says James Saggus, an AP man in Jackson, Miss. Many Southern newspapers accused the wire services of sensationalizing civil rights demonstrations in the early 1960s, and Northern editors later made the same complaint about coverage of urban riots.

In response, the AP has set up a "racial task force" of reporters who specialize in riot coverage. "They can be more accurate than other reporters, and they are less likely to panic in a tense situation," says Mr. Gallagher, the AP general manager. He concedes the AP has exaggerated some past demonstrations and strife.

The Associated Press has also formed a team of investigative reporters. The team, 10 reporters and an editor, has exposed Congressional nepotism, tax loopholes and pressures by coal interests against antipollution legislation. Stories on the Pentagon overpaying for M-16 rifles led Congress to close a loophole permitting such practices. An impressive amount of time and effort goes into such investigations. One reporter spent five months on a 10,000-word series on alleged corruption in highway construction. But editors killed the story as unfair, and the reporter, Bem Price, quit.

Holding good men is getting harder for both services, as it is for many newspapers. AP says turnover in its news operation has doubled in five years to 8% to 10% annually. AP alumni include David Lawrence, editor of U.S. News & World Report, and James Reston, executive editor of the New York Times. Television newscasters Walter Cronkite and David Brinkley both worked for United Press before it merged with the International News Service in 1958.

Besides using staffers and stringers, the Associated Press is entitled to use news stories written by local reporters of member papers. In theory, the AP gets exclusive use of these stories, even if the paper is also a UPI client. But in practice, UPI newsmen in many cities freely lift local stories from papers that have AP ties as well as from other papers and from broadcasters.

—A. KENT MACDOUGALL

1969

Obituaries:
Telling It Like It Was

DYING is no laughing matter. Yet when adman
Howard Luck Gossage lay dying of leukemia last
summer, he told a friend to get Jessica Mitford, author
of "The American Way of Death," to order his coffin.
"She's the only one who knows how to shop 'em," he
said.

This was all duly reported in Mr. Gossage's obituary in the New York Times, which was written by a
Times reporter who was a friend of Mr. Gossage. Writing the obituary was painful, says the reporter, Sidney
Zion. "I really loved Howard. It took me three martinis
and an hour and a half of staring at the typewriter to
get started."

The humor and the care—though perhaps not the
martinis—that went into the Times effort point up a
trend in the newspaper business that most readers and
newsmen alike applaud. In a small but growing number
of papers, obituaries are no longer just dull pieces written by green reporters or tired old-timers who seem to
be copying from a form. ("Born in Conesville, Mr. Webb
attended. . . .) Now, obituaries are among the best written, most informative stories in these papers. More im-

portant, they now seek to give a true picture of the dead man's life, touching on the bad as well as the good.

"We catch hell for bringing up" unpleasant episodes in an obituary, says Gordon Pates, managing editor of the San Francisco Chronicle, "but we feel it's part of the picture" of the dead man's life. In its obituary on actor James Dunn, Variety, the show business weekly, remarked that he had "a reputation as a heavy drinker." When singer Edith Piaf died, Variety related that she was reared by a grandmother who ran a brothel.

In its October obituary on Jack Kerouac, the New York Times said the novelist "increasingly eased his loneliness in drink." In its November obituary on Joseph P. Kennedy, the Times said that at one time "there were whispers that Mr. Kennedy was anti-Semitic." When W. Somerset Maugham died, the Times mentioned that the writer's "homosexuality was well known but excited little comment in the tolerant literary world of London."

The Times' main obituary writer, Alden Whitman, regularly interviews aging notables and prepares their obituaries in advance. Nearly all of his subjects seem flattered when he asks for an interview, he says. "They know they are going to die some day and they welcome the opportunity of talking about their life," he says. "They want to place some value on it and point up what they think is important—and what they want to be remembered for."

Mr. Whitman, a 56-year-old man who has been on the Times staff for 19 years, is not ghoulish about his work. "I like to see my stuff in print," he says, "but I don't sit around waiting for people to die." When he finishes an advance obituary, he says, "in my mind the subject has had it. I sort of lose track about who's dead and who's alive."

Mr. Whitman's own obituary, written by a col-

league, has been in the Times files since he suffered a
heart attack in 1965, but he hasn't ever bothered to read
it. "I won't be able to read it when it runs, and I'm not
interested in reading it now," he says. "I expect it will
be short and to the point." It is, say Times executives.
But they say it probably will be rewritten and made
more interesting and lively when Mr. Whitman does die.

Just by rating obituaries, Mr. Whitman and his
subjects are in a rather elite class. Metropolitan dailies
run obituaries on only 2% to 20% of the people in their
areas who die. "If a laborer dies at 99 or jumps off the
Golden Gate Bridge, we're interested," says Mr. Pates of
the San Francisco Chronicle. "But if he just dies in bed
of cirrhosis of the liver or something, we're not."

Most smaller papers try to run obituaries on everyone who dies in their areas, but these obituaries are
often just perfunctory stories that don't even tell the
cause of death. Cancer kills one of six Americans. But
small papers often refer to the disease only as a "linger-
ing illness" or with some other euphemism, primarily
because relatives don't like to disclose that a person died
of cancer. The American Cancer Society, as part of its
educational campaign against the disease, has asked
newspapers to mention the illness in obituaries and
more and more are doing so.

While some relatives don't want to list the cause of
death, others are leery of listing the address of the de-
ceased. There's a good reason for that. Obituaries and
paid death notices are among the best read parts of a
paper, and the readers include burglars who like to pay
their respects by visiting the home of the dead person
during the funeral. (Real estate agents also are avid
readers of obituaries, hoping to find a widow who wants
to sell her home.)

Some people can't even rate an obituary in a small
paper. In Lynchburg, Va., both The News and The Ad-

vance will accept paid death notices for both Negroes and whites, but obituaries on ordinary residents are restricted to whites. Carter Glass III, the papers' general manager, says the policy dates back to 1840, when slavery was still legal, and he says he adheres to it because "I believe in the judgment of my forebears, and this is what the vast majority of our readers want."

Mr. Glass says, however, that the papers are willing to report the death of a few "newsworthy" Negroes. And, indeed, some years ago the papers did prominently play the death of a Negro who had worked for the papers for more than 40 years. "He was one of the finest gentlemen I've ever known. He never asked for a raise," says Mr. Glass, though he can't recall the gentleman's last name.

Children, except those from prominent families, also seldom receive obituaries, especially in big metropolitan papers. The Associated Press has 650 advance obituaries prepared, including one for the racehorse Kelso, but there isn't a child in the group. "What can you say about them?" asks obituary editor Douw H. Fonda.

The AP's 650 obituaries, which it calls "biographical sketches," run from Abbott, George, stage director, to Zukor, Adolph, motion picture producer. Each month the AP mails a batch of new advance obituaries and updates old ones. The December batch included obituaries on Cabinet member Robert Finch, Rhodesian Prime Minister Ian Smith and ultraconservative clergyman Carl McIntyre and an updated version of the "sketch" on author Anne Morrow Lindbergh.

Some notables die before Mr. Fonda can get around to them. Robert Lehman, financier and art collector, "led a fascinating life and deserved a sketch," says Mr. Fonda. But Mr. Lehman died on Aug. 9, before Mr.

Fonda had time to prepare one. "You can't win them all," he sighs.

Some newspapers put these advance obituaries in type, but others don't. "There's sort of a feeling that it's bad luck" to put an obituary in type, says Jack Driscoll, assistant to the editor of the Boston Globe. As a result, the Globe doesn't have any obituaries of local notables in type, though it apparently doesn't mind putting a curse on out-of-towners and has set in type the obituaries of 30 national and international figures.

If having your obituary put in type is bad luck, having it appear in the paper would seem to be really ominous. That's what lawyer Nathaniel Taylor thought when he read his own obituary in 1955 in Newsday, a Long Island newspaper. The paper had been hoaxed by a man who Mr. Taylor suspects was a client's disgruntled ex-husband. Mr. Taylor wasn't a bit amused, however, and the subject still rankles him. He declines to discuss the matter now, nearly 15 years after it happened, complaining that any further mention could really be "the kiss of death."

Ernest Hemingway also lived to see his obituary printed. He was hurt in two plane crashes in Africa in 1953 and was reported dead. Many newspapers ran obituaries before the news that he wasn't dead reached them. "There were certain inaccuracies and many good things were said that were in no way deserved," he later said. "Most of the obituaries I could never have written nearly as well myself."

Some people actually have the chance to write their own. James M. Langley, onetime ambassador to Pakistan and later the editor of the Concord, N.H., Monitor, was one. The day after his death in 1968, the Monitor's lead story on page one carried his byline.

It began: "I died late yesterday afternoon."

1970   —A. KENT MACDOUGALL

Variety:
Bible of Broadway

SPICE is the life of Variety. The show business weekly consistently bites the hand that feeds it. It deflates show business' inflated egos and inflated box-office receipts. It prints the embarrassing and the confidential. (One requirement for a job as a reporter for Variety, says a television network official, "is to be able to read a memo upside down on someone's desk.") It calls 'em as it sees 'em, and it doesn't see everything the way the industry would like.

"We trample on toes," says Robert J. Landry, managing editor.

But if Variety isn't loved, it is read. It is the first thing many show business types turn to each Wednesday. Alexander H. Cohen, a Broadway producer who has had his personal quarrels with the publication, schedules his frequent trips to Europe for Wednesdays "so I can take Variety along." Mr. Cohen says he gets "enormous pleasure reading it without interruption the entire six hours to London." Nat Lefkowitz, executive vice president of William Morris Agency Inc., a big talent agency, says, "Variety is essential reading."

It's essential because it really tells what's happening. It is jam-packed with news and reviews of show business doings from New York to Moscow, from Des Moines, Iowa, to Salonika, Greece. It seems to have tipsters everywhere. The Motion Picture Association of America has repeatedly been embarrassed by Variety stories based on confidential memos from the association to its members. Fed up, association President Jack Valenti—whose former boss has had trouble with press leaks, too—sent a confidential memo pleading with members to keep all memos confidential. Someone leaked that one to Variety, too.

The paper also keeps weekly tab on how stage shows and movies are faring across the country. Some producers refuse to disclose box-office figures, but Variety always seems to get them one way or another. Some give inflated figures, and Variety prints these—next to the real ones that it has ferreted out.

The weekly figures fascinate showmen and investors by pinpointing trends in public acceptance—movie by movie, play by play, city by city. To others, the reports can be incomprehensible. A recent report of Chicago, for instance, was headlined:

Chi Off Sharply But 'Miracle' Fair
$17,000, '1,000 Dolls' Socko 10 G, 3d;
'Luke' Boff 34G, 'Camelot' 40G, 8th

And the story started: "Windy City deluxer biz dipped sharply this frame, as firstrun houses mark time with aging holdovers. Monroe duo of 'The Temptress' and 'Many Ways' looks tidy on opener." A partial translation: The movie business that week wasn't very good in Chicago, although the movie "House of 1,000 Dolls" took in an impressive $10,000 in box office receipts in its third week of showing—or, as the story said, in its "third Loop lap."

The pictureless tabloid does have a way with words. In Varietyese, a Western movie is a "sagebrusher," "oater" or "they-went-that-awayer." Downtown movie

theaters are "grind de luxers," neighborhood movie
houses are "nabes" and burlesque houses are "peel par-
lors." The head of a company is the "prez" or "topper."
A child actor is a "juve," a music composer a "cleffer," a
magician a "hocus-pocuser" and a soap-opera star a
"suds churner." In 1929, when the stock market
crashed, Variety headlined it, WALL STREET LAYS AN
EGG. And in 1935, over a story about Midwestern mov-
iegoers shunning pictures about rural life, the headline
was: STIX NIX HICK PIX.

"It's our own glib way of colorfully stating the
case," says Abel Green, the 67-year-old editor who is colorful in his own right. Mr. Green, who has been with Variety since 1918, is a small man who favors bow ties,
flashes wads of $100 bills, talks fast and frequents such
celebrity-haunted New York watering holes as Dinty
Moore's, Twenty-One and Toots Shor's.

Mr. Green knows just about everybody worth knowing in show business. He calls Groucho Marx by his
"square handle" of Julius. He once had a dispute with
old crony Walter Winchell, who referred to the Variety
editor as Unable Green, but they have since made up
and Variety now runs Mr. Winchell's column. Mr. Winchell, who has been yearning for a New York outlet
since the World Journal Tribune folded, doesn't charge
Variety.

With the freedom to say what you want and the
chance to hobnob with the stars, it would seem that Variety would be a pleasant place to work. It is, say many
of the two dozen newsmen on the publication, but they
are quick to cite the disadvantages. The hours are long,
they say, the pay is low and the office is cramped. But,
says reporter Jack Pitman, "This is a great place for a
neurotic to splatter his psyche."

Variety is housed in a five-story, 20-foot-wide building in the middle of the theater district in midtown New

York. The editors and reporters are jammed into one shabby room. The walls, pencils and stationery are green. "And that's my color when I hear about salaries on other papers," says Hobe Morrison, a critic and reporter. A good newsman at Variety makes $200 or so a week, former employes say, considerably below what a top reporter or editor makes on other publications in New York.

Editor Green and publisher and principal owner Syd Silverman sit at battered, back-to-back desks on a platform in the newsroom. They look out a window at 46th Street. A drunken actor once fired a shot through the window at Mr. Silverman's grandfather, Sime Silverman, who founded Variety in 1905. Sime—his last name is seldom used, even in print—ran the publication until his death in 1933. Just before his death he founded an offshoot, Daily Variety, which is still published weekdays in Hollywood; it is a slim paper that concentrates on movie news for West Coast readers.

Low pay and stray gunshots aren't the major problems in working at Variety, though. The biggest problem, reporters say, is getting the hypersensitive people in show business to tell you the truth. "If you think there's a credibility gap in Washington, you ought to cover this business," says reporter Jack Pitman. "We have been lied to so frequently, by almost everybody, that if a tipster we trust assures us that a report is solidly based rather than rumor, we go with it. Eight times out of ten, we're right."

Editor Abel Green concedes his reporters often don't check out rumors before printing them. But he defends the practice. "If you try to check," he says, "the company will undercut you by denying it or sending it out as a press handout."

Variety's reporters and the people they write about both claim to be misunderstood. At the television networks, officials "always want you to make nice," complains TV editor Les Brown. "When you don't, they impute all kinds of base motives to the story. They assume I have a bad hate on for them, and someone at another network fed me the poison." (Mr. Brown criticizes all TV networks impartially. Last fall he wrote: "The three tv webs have laid a mighty egg this season.")

On the other hand, Howard Coleman, press relations director of A. C. Nielsen Co., which compiles audience ratings on TV programs, says Variety just doesn't understand the ratings business. "What kind of funny numbers are you hoking up this week?" is the attitude of Variety reporters who call A. C. Nielsen, Mr. Coleman says. "They're doing the industry a disservice" by prematurely judging the success or failure of shows from early ratings, he says. "It infuriates us."

Answers Mr. Brown: "We have not treated Nielsen the way Nielsen wants to be treated."

The weekly edition, which costs 50 cents and usually runs 64 to 80 or more pages, uses the services of 200 stringers, who review local nightclub acts, road shows and anything else in town. The reviews aren't always prophetic.

Fred Tew, Variety's man in Detroit, reviewed Fiddler on the Roof when it was trying out there. Mr. Tew, a Chrysler Corp. public relations man, said Fiddler was "no smash hit, no blockbuster," but he allowed it "may have a chance for a moderate success on Broadway." The show, of course, turned out to be a smash hit and a blockbuster.

Broadwayites aren't always happy about the out-of-town notices. Says Harvey Sabinson, press agent for many Broadway shows: "It's a woeful responsibility for a man making $5 to $10 a review to pass judgment on a $500,000 musical."

Mr. Sabinson is wrong on one count. The reviewers

seldom get $5 for their efforts. U.S. stringers are paid $5
per column, and overseas correspondents get $6. But re-
views seldom run a full column. It's not money, but love
for show business—and free admission into movies and
nightclubs—that motivates most stringers. "It's a fun
job," says Mr. Tew of Detroit. "I meet a great number of
very interesting, very alive people." He admits his guess
on Fiddler was wrong, but he says, "My overall batting
average is pretty high."

Most movie and many nightclub reviews are written by the full-time staff in New York and Hollywood.
Nightclub reviews are seldom harsh, but a bad movie is
called bad. Operation Kid Brother, "the latest 007 imi-
tation . . . is so unbelievably inept that many viewers
may find it hilarious fun," wrote one Variety critic. Another dismissed Sadismo, a "shockumentary" about
cruelty to men and animals, as "cincmatic trash," reporting that one voice in the audience at the double feature yelled, "Show de uddah pickchuh!"

—A. KENT MACDOUGALL

1968

Trade Journals:
Biased and Bland

IT used to be called Corset & Underwear Review, but now it's named Body Fashions. It's a trade publication for merchants of underwear, and it often presents paid ads as editorial copy. "The reader is looking for educational information, and it can better be disseminated as editorial copy," explains John B. Gellatly, president of the Harcourt Brace Jovanovich subsidiary that publishes Body Fashions and 22 other trade journals.

There's nothing unusual about the practice, Mr. Gellatly says, and critics of the press say, alas, that's all too true. There is much that is disreputable in American journalism, these critics say, but many of the specialized business, technical and professional publications that constitute the trade press are the most disreputable of all. Many charge for editorial space and tie ads to copy. Often, their editors sell ads—and their ad salesmen help edit.

Most trade publications automatically defend the industries they cover. Consider, for example, America's Textile Reporter, a magazine that bills itself as "the most powerful influence in the textile industry." Byssinosis is the brown lung disease that an estimated 100,-000 present or former American textile workers have contracted from inhaling cotton dust, but to America's Textile Reporter byssinosis is "a thing thought up by venal doctors who attended" a 1968 International Labor Organization meeting in Africa, "where inferior races are bound to be afflicted by new diseases more superior people defeated years ago."

Such outbursts are admittedly rare in a field usually criticized more for blandness than strong words. And even the harshest critics of the trade press are quick to concede that there are many top-quality publications: McGraw-Hill's Chemical Week and Modern Hospital are among those often cited. But they maintain there are far more bad ones among the nation's nearly 2,400 trade publications.

The best publications are very good, and editors and publishers of these take pains to dissociate themselves from the bad ones. They say it's as unfair to lump the entire trade press together under one label as it is to include sex tabloids with the New York Times, when rating the U.S. general-interest press. Charles S. Mill, president of the American Business Press, an organization of 515 trade journals, worries that the entire trade press is often unfairly judged "by the fleabag outfits published in somebody's garage."

No one is sure just how widespread the questionable practices are. A 1964 survey by the Society of Business Magazine Editors (now the American Society of Business Press Editors) found that of 76 publications queried 55% said their ad salesmen exerted "some" influence in selecting and researching stories. And 22% acknowledged that it was accepted policy on their magazines "to give preference to advertisers when gathering information for articles."

William S. Miller, president of the group, says a similar survey today probably would produce similar results. "I have sensed no great difference since 1964 in the practices and attitudes of the editors I know," he says.

In 1967 the American Business Press surveyed 43 editors and found that a third of them actively solicited advertising. The group reported the results in its magazine, Better Editing. The article, entitled "Editorial Ethics Aren't," argued that editorial ethics "are what any editor owes his boss in return for his salary"—but that providing good service to readers isn't a matter of ethics at all, but simply sound business. The article concluded: "In business publishing, the readers rarely pay for the product, and pay only a fraction of the real cost when they do buy subscriptions. Since they do not pay, or pay very little, nothing is owed them."

Mr. Mill, the president of the organization, seems embarrassed by the article. "I wish they (the authors) hadn't said that," he now says.

While Mr. Miller of the American Society of Business Press Editors says he can see little change in editorial ethics in the past seven years, that view could be questioned. With the recession cutting into advertising, publishers of many trade journals seem to have become more obsequious than ever—or at least more careful to avoid angering news sources and advertisers.

Advertising in the journals has been declining. Of McGraw-Hill's 33 U.S. trade journals, 30 lost ads pages in 1970, for instance. But for many trade journals, the advertising slump began long before the general economic decline. Total trade journal ad pages peaked in 1957. In 1969, trade journals' share of total advertising expenditures declined to 3.9% from 4.4% five years earlier, McCann-Erickson Inc., the ad agency, estimates.

Faced with these facts, the trade journals are anxious to please. When Jessica Mitford wrote a scathing piece in Atlantic magazine last July assailing the advertising and sales practices of Famous Writers School, Di-

Trade Journals: Biased and Bland 133

rect Marketing magazine assailed Atlantic for striking "a cruel blow." "We think it's a shame that Jessica Mitford wasted her time hurting the feelings of so many dedicated people," Direct Marketing editorialized. Delighted, the dedicated people at Famous Writers School sent reprints of the editorial to newspapers, security analysts and others.

Though Famous Writers didn't pay Direct Marketing for the reprints, some publications make money by charging handsomely for rights to reprint paeans. Without reprint income in 1970, says Elizabeth M. Manning, owner and publisher of Finance magazine, "we would have just about scratched by." Among Finance's reprint customers last year was Mack Trucks Inc., which was so pleased with Finance's cover story on Mack chairman Zenon C. R. Hansen that it bought 10,000 copies of the magazine at $2 each.

Even with reprint income, though, some magazines have been unable to stay alive in recent years. The less-than-2,400 trade publications now available are down significantly in number from 2,548 five years ago.

During the recession year of 1970, Harcourt Brace Jovanovich folded four trade publications and sold a fifth, and Crowell Collier & Macmillan Inc., Chilton Co. and Ziff-Davis Publishing Co. each discontinued two. Some others are losing so much money they won't be able to stay alive much longer. A few journals still make after-tax profits of 20%, but a confidential survey of 217 journals made by an accounting firm for the American Business Press found that fully a third operated at a loss in 1969. Of journals with annual volume of less than $250,000, more than half lost money, the survey found.

Some people, even within the profession, think there still are too many trade journals around. Mr. Mill of the American Business Press says, "There are nearly twice as many trade journals as there ought to be—both commercial journals and those put out by nonprofit associations." He thinks "the strong ones will get stronger and a lot of the weak ones are going to go out of business."

Trade journals have proliferated because publishing appeals to many people and because initial capital investment is low, Mr. Mill says. Many journals keep going by keeping costs and ad rates low. "Fringe trade journals exist because their ad rates are low enough and their nuisance value is high enough that people put up with them," says William Marsteller, chairman of Marsteller Inc., an ad agency that leads all others in placing ads in trade journals.

Howard G. Sawyer, a Marsteller vice president, says advertisers often support state and regional trade journals "for political reasons—to keep peace with a local sales manager or an association of dealers—rather than for advertising values."

Many trade journals make no bones about putting the interests of their advertisers ahead of readers. At Record World, "our function is to help the manufacturer expose his product to our readers," says publisher Bob Austin. The weekly's Oct. 17 issue did just that in a big way for the Decca Records division of MCA Inc. In exchange for 17 pages of advertising, Record World ran seven pages of glowing articles and pictures on Decca.

Was the reader aware of this tie-in? Replies Mr. Austin: "It would be awfully hard not to realize that the editorial was there because of the advertising."

Record World doesn't charge for such editorial puffery, but a competitor, Billboard, does. Billboard ran 16 special sections in 1970, up from nine in 1969, on record companies and performers. Typically, the sections contain two to three pages of obvious advertising to each page of what editor-in-chief Lee Zhito calls "simulated editorial, or advertorial," which is also paid advertising. Some sections in Billboard are labeled "sponsored" and some aren't. Four recent sections without a "sponsored" disclaimer ranged from a 12-page "Salute to Heintje," a 14-year-old Dutch singer, to a 40-page section on the record division of American Broadcasting Cos.

Ron Carpenter, Billboard sales director, says the omission of disclaimers is "an absolute goof" caused by "mechanical mistakes." He defends the special sections as a "legitimate hype" (a term meaning hard-sell promotion) and says some second-rate performers who have sought such sections have been turned down.

(The company or performer being profiled doesn't usually buy all the ads in Billboard's special sections. Some are paid for by business associates and friends. One ad in a 22-page spread on Buck Owens, for example, was taken by the singer's "personal friend" Ronald Reagan. One of the ads in a section commemorating the 21st anniversary of Barclay Records effused: "Our warmest congratulations on your 20th anniversary.")

Readers of many journals recognize they are mainly reading puff stories, so they balk at paying much—sometimes at paying anything—for the publications. This, plus pressure from advertisers to reach top decision-makers, has prompted some journals to switch partly or wholly to free distribution. Finance magazine, for instance, which says it has a circulation of 57,000 (the magazine had "a big fight" with the Audit Bureau of Circulations and quit that group), gives away 15,000 of those copies each month.

Most of the best journals still charge their readers, however, and some of the charges are quite steep. The American Banker, for instance, recently raised its subscription price to $150 a year from $100.

Many reporters and editors on general-interest

newspapers and magazines read trade publications regularly to keep up with the news. While many publications pour out editorials in support of their industries, some also cover the news in those industries thoroughly and accurately. Broadcasting and Aviation Week & Space Technology fit into this category. But while these reporters and editors crib from the trade publications, they often feel sorry for their lower-paid colleagues who work for the trade press. Some other people, however, say the trade press gets what it pays for.

"Low-paid, incompetent reporters are common," asserts John Manfredi, news bureau manager for General Foods Corp. and a former reporter for Fairchild Publications Inc. (Fairchild likes to look on Women's Wear Daily and its other publications as newspapers rather than trade publications, but not everyone agrees.) "Most trade journal editors wouldn't be allowed on a daily newspaper," Mr. Manfredi claims, though he says he has high regard for a few.

Like many companies, General Foods discourages executives from granting an interview to a trade journalist without the right to review the article before it's published. Mr. Manfredi and other public relations men defend the right of review as guaranteeing accuracy, but trade journalists tend to regard it as quasi-censorship, and the best of them seldom go along with this.

Public relations men generally accept as a fact of life that they have a better chance of getting a publicity release published in a trade journal if their client is also an advertiser. "A number of editors have candidly told me, 'It's a hell of a good story, but . . .'" says Jack Bernstein, who runs a public relations agency in New York. His conclusion: "Trade journals would love to be pure, but they cut corners to stay alive."

U.S. Industrial Publications Inc. of Stamford, Conn., avoids hassles with nonadvertisers by having a firm rule that it will run stories only about companies that advertise. The company's five quarterly journals guarantee advertisers (which include General Electric Co. and Chrysler Corp.) that their ads won't face ads for competitive products. In return for this exclusivity, the advertisers pay the same page rates for articles about their products as for straight ads.

"The articles are often less promotional than those found in traditional trade magazines—the sell is often softer," claims Howard A. Reed, president of U.S. Industrial Publications. "Unlike many traditional trade magazines, we don't make any bones about collusion with advertisers. And we never run a puff piece on a potential advertiser."

Some traditional trade journals run publicity handouts from nonadvertisers as well as advertisers, but levy a $15 to $25 "engraving charge" for each published photograph. The Rocky Mountain Food Dealer averages a profit of $12 on each $20 engraving charge. "This type of charge has become part of the survival of our type of publication," says Charles M. Knapp Jr., publisher, editor and advertising manager of the monthly and executive director of the Rocky Mountain Food Dealers Association, which puts it out. (Associations publish a third of all journals.)

Other publications economize in other ways. Some, like many newspapers, let news sources pay for reporters' reporting trips. Others have been cutting back on their staffs. America's Textile Reporter, for instance, recently dismissed its Washington columnist to save money, but still runs a column entitled "Reporter in Washington." It's written now by a staffer who phones sources in the capital from the magazine's offices in Greenville, S.C.

—A. KENT MACDOUGALL

1971

Penal Press:
A Behind-Bars View

GENE Stees writes for a captive audience.
    Literally.

Mr. Stees is editor of OPNews, a weekly tabloid written and published by and for the inmates at the Ohio Penitentiary in Columbus. OPNews' forte is local coverage. Its six pages concentrate on cell block gossip ("Killer Green has a new hobby these days, raising babies—canaries, that is"), "campus" sports, editorials on law enforcement, comings and goings and other community news.

Freedom of the press doesn't exactly reign at OPNews. Prison powers have banned stories about God, Vietnam and Black Power, subjects that could foment fights among the readership. Editors and writers never travel on official business (though an occasional staffer at some prison papers tries to escape), and even outside phone calls are banned. In the best journalistic tradition, though, the pay is low. Editor Stees earns 8½ cents an hour. (Staffers without dependents earn 4 cents an hour; Mr. Stees, a former professor of education at Ohio University, is serving a life sentence for killing his wife, but he has two children who are dependents).

OPNews is one of the liveliest of the nation's prison periodicals. Some papers in this backwater of the Fourth Estate aren't more than mimeographed newsletters. Some are issued irregularly, as talent and printing facilities permit. But a surprising number are well-written, professional-looking publications that come out punctually every week, fortnight or month.

Russell N. Baird, professor of journalism at Ohio University (where he once was a colleague of Mr. Stees) and author of The Penal Press, counts 222 prison periodicals, up from 85 in 1945. Nearly two-thirds of the 200,000 or so inmates in Federal and state correctional institutions now have their own publications, Mr. Baird says.

Prison administrators value the publications. For one thing, the papers give the administrators a means of communicating with their charges. Some wardens even write columns for the papers. The papers also provide the inmates with a forum for their writing talents —and with a place to blow off steam.

The newspapers can sometimes be effective instruments for convicts to bring about prison reform. The papers are wielding more and more influence as an increasing number of sociologists, penologists, legislators, jurists and others concerned with reform join the subscription rolls. Mr. Baird estimates that outsiders account a third of the penal press's total circulation.

The rising number of outsiders reading the publications has turned some wardens into censors, however. Joseph R. Brierley, superintendent of the Pennsylvania Correctional Institute at Philadelphia, killed the April issue of the Eastern Echo because it was devoted entirely to sex in prison. The issue was "trash," he says, because it "dealt in specifics" about homosexual affairs.

"This could have a bad effect on mothers, wives and sweethearts of prisoners," he says.

Most prisons won't let the papers discuss civil rights, religion or politics. "Anything that might be inflammatory and start arguments among the inmates is out," says Troy Harris, an official at Ohio Penitentiary. Derogatory references to prisoners are taboo in Texas. "If an inmate has a deformed nose, we don't want him referred to as 'Hose Nose'—he has enough troubles as it is," says W. D. Kutach, an official of the Texas Department of Corrections. No such restrictions hampered the first issue of Pennsylvania Correctional Institute's Eastern Echo last winter, though. It mentioned "Jake the Snake," "John the Horse," "Crazy Charlie" and "Goony Walsh."

There are other differences between penal publications and the daily press. Some wardens bar photoengraving equipment lest it be used to forge $10 bills as well as make pictures of the weightlifting team. "We're trying to teach these men good habits, not bad habits," says E. L. Maxwell, warden at Ohio Penitentiary. The rare picture in OPNews is engraved outside the prison.

And the convict journalists sometimes encounter deadline difficulties that their outside brothers never face. The biweekly San Quentin (Calif.) News missed a January issue because of what Warden Lawrence E. Wilson called a riotous situation. Some publications cease when a key employe's time is up. The monthly Menard Time was late with several issues this year because two printers tried to escape, prompting the warden to end night work in the print shop.

—A. KENT MACDOUGALL

1967

Unethical

Newspaper Practices

IN Boston and Chicago, newspaper investigations into suspected hanky-panky suddenly are aborted. In one case, a subject of inquiry turns out to be a stockholder of the paper and a friend of the publisher. In the other, the investigation threatens to embarrass a politician who could help the paper in a building project.

In California, a batch of small newspapers run editorials endorsing the Detroit position on auto safety. All are worded similarly. An incredible coincidence, this identity not only of opinion but of phrasing? Hardly, for all the articles are drawn from a single "canned" editorial emanating from an advertising agency in San Francisco.

In Denver, the advertising staff of a big daily wrestles with an arithmetic problem. A big advertiser has been promised news stories and pictures amounting to 25% of the ad space it buys; the paper already has run hundreds of column inches of glowing prose but is still not close to the promised allotment of "news" and now is running out of nice things to say.

All this hardly enhances the image of objectivity and fierce independence the U.S. press tries so hard to project. Yet talks with scores of reporters, editors, pub-

141

lishers, public relations men and others reveal that practices endangering—and often subverting—newspaper integrity are more common than the man on the street might dream. Result: The buyer who expects a dime's worth of truth every time he picks up his paper often is short-changed.

All newspapers, including this one, must cope with the blandishments and pressures of special interests who seek distortion or omission of the truth. And no newspaper, again including this one, can ever be positive that every one of its staff always resists these blandishments and pressures. But on some papers, the trouble starts at the top; it is the publisher himself who lays down news policies designed to aid one group or attack another.

Those publishers who do strive to report the news fully and impartially—and their number appears to be growing—have been taking several steps in recent years to make unethical or questionable behavior less likely on the part of their newsmen.

They have boosted editorial salaries sharply, thus making staffers less susceptible to bribes and favors offered by outsiders and reducing their dependence on outside work—which can, and sometimes does, result in conflict of interest. And more papers are laying down rules that forbid or discourage practices they consider unhealthy.

All in all, there is considerable evidence that "the ethics of the American press are probably at the highest level now in the history of the press anywhere," as claimed by Russell E. Hurst, executive officer of Sigma Delta Chi, the professional journalism society. But this is not the same thing as saying they are uniformly high; the press may have come a long way in recent years, but interviews disclose it has a long, hard climb to go before reaching any summit of ethical purity.

Ideally, a newspaper is supposed to pluck out the truth from the daily maelstrom of events, make independent and objective judgments as to its importance to readers, and print it without fear or favor. Resistance to outside pressures, including those applied by advertisers, is considered a must.

It is plain, however, that a sizable minority of newspapers still are putty in the hands of their advertisers, that they allow personal as well as business considerations to flavor the news to a marked degree, that their salaries are low and that they tolerate staff practices hardly conducive to editorial independence and objectivity.

The discerning reader sometimes can tell when a newspaper is "puffing" a favored advertiser or other outsider, but it is much harder to detect the sins of omission—the legitimate story suppressed, the investigation scotched for fear of offending someone. Readers of the Chicago Tribune, for example, probably never realized why one crusade against a truck licensing scandal faded from that paper this year.

The reporter in this case was Pulitzer prize winner George Bliss, who last year revealed that trucks engaging solely in intrastate commerce within Illinois were using cheap out-of-state licenses in order to avoid paying the relatively high fees required for Illinois plates.

The Tribune, proud of the exposes, boasted: "Illegal out-of-state truck licenses were costing Illinois millions in lost taxes . . . until the Chicago Tribune exposed the racket." Or so read a front-cover ad in the July 23, 1966, issue of Editor & Publisher. The Tribune's attitude changed markedly, however, after McCormick Place burned down in January of this year.

The lakefront exhibition and convention hall was a mammoth monument to the memory of the late Col. Robert McCormack, who for so long guided the destiny of the Tribune. The paper naturally was eager to gather the financial and political support necessary to have the hall rebuilt and expanded, and after the fire Tribune Editor W. D. Maxwell met with exhibition hall officials to see what could be done. Also at the meeting was Paul Powell, Secretary of State of Illinois.

Mr. Powell is said to have great influence with some members of the state legislature, which subsequently voted state funds to help finance the hall's rebuilding (two such bills are before the governor now). Also, Mr. Powell's office had jurisdiction over truck licensing. Reporter Bliss already had disclosed that Mr. Powell's chief investigator had a criminal record, a story resulting in the immediate resignation of the investigator and the claim by Mr. Powell that he didn't know about his aide's background. At the time of the fire, Mr. Bliss was working on leads to another story that might have proved embarrassing to Mr. Powell's department—but shortly after the fire and the subsequent meeting, Mr. Bliss was told to lay off.

Was a deal made, the Tribune agreeing to stifle its investigation in exchange for whatever help Mr. Powell could give in gathering support for the rebuilding of McCormick Place? Though he refuses to talk to The Wall Street Journal, it is known that reporter Bliss was enraged by the order to halt his inquiry and flatly declared there was a deal between the two. Other sources say there was, too. Another possibility: That there was no definite quid pro quo, only a decision by the Tribune to avoid offending a politician whose help might prove valuable.

Editor Maxwell says he made no deal with Mr. Powell and scoffs at the idea that the official has enough political pull to make such an agreement worthwhile.

Such blackouts of news involving newspapers are quite common; hardly a working journalist could deny that one of the gravest weaknesses in coverage exhibited by the American press is its coverage of itself. This became apparent in Philadelphia recently when Harry Karafin, a prize-winning investigative reporter for the Inquirer and a staffer for nearly 30 years, was arrested on charges of blackmail and extortion. Philadelphia magazine, not a local newspaper, printed the first blast at Karafin in its April issue.

From then until the reporter's arrest earlier this month, the rival Philadelphia Bulletin carried not a word on the case—even though the Inquirer itself (which claims it had repeatedly pursued tips about Mr. Karafin's activities but could not prove anything) fired him shortly before the magazine expose and carried the whole story afterward.

More often newspapers try to cover up when unfavorable news breaks about their own operations. A few years ago the Clarion-Ledger and Daily News, jointly owned papers in Jackson, Miss., were hauled into court by U.S. officials on charges dealing with violations of Federal laws governing overtime pay. The court action resulted in a permanent injunction barring the papers from continuing the offending practices. Not a word of all this appeared in the Jackson papers; staffers were even ordered to stay away from the court, and they did.

News blackouts aren't always limited to a paper's problems. Sometimes they make unpersons out of individuals who somehow have come into bad odor with the paper. On the Philadelphia Inquirer, for example, a blacklist of names not to appear in print is believed to have long existed. News executives at the paper say there hasn't been any such list, to their knowledge, but many Quaker City newsmen find that hard to believe.

So might Gaylord P. Harnwell, president of the University of Pennsylvania. Though a newsmaker by the very virtue of his position, his name regularly was expunged from the Inquirer and its sister publication, the Philadelphia Daily News, roughly from December 1963 into March 1964. All the while, his name was appearing in stories printed by the rival Bulletin. On one occasion, when Mr. Harnwell called for an extensive survey of athletics at Penn in a letter to an annual alumni banquet, the Inquirer attributed the letter to "a high university official."

This went on until Philadelphia magazine, which broke the Karafin story, drew attention to the blackout. The reason for it is still a mystery; Inquirer officials blandly deny a blackout was ordered and Mr. Harnwell's office won't discuss the matter.

Discovery that a staffer is "on the take" is, of course, ground for immediate dismissal at any paper with the least respect for honesty. By their very nature, though, such arrangements between reporters and outsiders are clandestine and hard for a paper to uncover.

In the vast majority of instances, however, the reporter is honestly employed by outside interests with the knowledge of his newspaper bosses (but not the public who reads his articles). Often the reason is low pay on the paper; a reporter for the Jackson, Miss., papers says: "Almost everybody here does some kind of outside work. With the salaries they pay, you have to." Pay scales at the Clarion-Ledger and Daily News are guarded like atomic secrets, but staffers put the range at roughly $65 to $150 a week for reporters. In the past employes have labored at such sidelines as making slogan-bearing license plates and running photography studios.

There's little chance of conflict of interest in jobs like these. But there are numerous examples of outside work by newsmen that clearly could prejudice their coverage of certain stories.

On some papers, courthouse reporters have been

appointed by courts as estate appraisers. Are they in a
position to write critically of the courts if the facts dictate it, considering they might be risking the loss of
their outside income? For the same reason, how much
objectivity in rail strike coverage could have been expected from the labor reporter of a sizable East Coast
daily—who until recently had an outside publicity job
with a major railroad?

Some highly respected veteran reporters are in the
same position. In January, for example, Bob Considine
wrote a column brushing off Detroit's auto safety critics
and championing the position of the embattled manufacturers. What of it, considering Mr. Considine has
every right to his own opinion? Nothing, except that
he also was being paid for appearing in and narrating a
Ford Motor Co. movie on its auto safety research and
engineering. There's no secret about Mr. Considine's
work for Ford—it was publicized—but it was not mentioned in the column.

Junketing also is widely viewed as a threat to objectivity, but is widely practiced nonetheless. Junkets are
trips by reporters whose travel and other expenses are
paid by the news source, not the newspaper. The source
often stages some "event" or shows off some facility of
marginal interest, to give the reporters some excuse for
going, but the real intent in many cases is to maintain
good relations with the press as well as to garner some
publicity in the process.

These junkets sometimes are little more than bac-
chanals for attending newsmen. Reporters still recall
with relish a Caribbean trip staged by one big company
a few years ago; the firm bankrolled everything, including the services of a bevy of prostitutes. On one stopover
during the return trip, some of the more rambunctious
journalists were jailed by the police, and company attorneys used their good offices to get them sprung

("These are very important editors from New York. . . .").

The "news" stories that emerge from such affairs are almost always complimentary, if not gushing, and almost always have little or no intrinsic worth. Some editors frankly admit this, and say they use junkets mainly as a way to give deserving staffers expense-paid vacations.

Such measures, however, actually do little to correct another grave fault of a good many papers: Favoritism toward business in general and advertisers in particular. Indeed, it seems apparent that a double standard exists at many papers; reporters and editors are expected to eschew practices that might compromise the paper's integrity, while the paper itself, by actual policy or common practice, distorts the news to suit advertisers or literally hands over news space to them.

At the Herald-News, an 80,000-circulation daily in Passaic-Clifton, N.J., outside jobs that might constitute conflict of interest are frowned on; the paper once ordered a staffer to give up a $50-a-month job writing news releases for the Clifton Red Cross. Yet once a week the paper carries a "weekly business review" page comprised of ads and a "news story" about an advertiser—a story contracted for by the advertiser when he buys his ad space. The stories are uniformly complimentary. "Everybody's the greatest," says Managing Editor Arthur G. McMahon.

The Dallas Times Herald does much the same thing, printing each Monday from 2½ to 3 pages of "commercial, industrial news of Dallas." The "news" coverage of each company depends on how much ad space it buys; an eight-inch ad run weekly for a year, for example, qualifies for eight pictures and eight stories throughout that year, whether there is anything significant to report or not.

Jack Padgett Sr., who produces the page for the paper (he is not a staffer but an independent contractor), claims, however, that his product is one of the most successful of its kind in the country "because we try to make every story as newsy as possible."

The general interests of the business community, rather than those of a specific advertiser, also affect news content. To the Sacramento Bee, for example, the weather never is hot, even when you can fry an egg on the pavement. The most the paper will concede is that it is "unseasonably warm." Anything stronger might scare off prospective new business and industry, it's felt.

Some time ago Boston papers also fudged on the weather reports; when a deluge was on the way, the papers would tell readers there was a "possibility of showers." Heavy rains, of course, are bad for the retail trade.

There is evidence that many once-principled newsmen have been deeply demoralized by their papers' surrender to advertisers' interests. A recent survey of 162 business and financial editors, for example, revealed that 22.6% of them "indicated that as a matter of routine they were compelled to puff up or alter and downgrade business stories at the request of the advertisers." The survey found that "such pressure is most effective when it is brought to bear through the publication's own advertising department."

Prof. Timothy Hubbard of the University of Missouri, who conducted the survey, says many editors object strenuously to such attempts at distortion but often lack backing from higher management. "As a result," he says, "some seem curiously resigned to trimming their editorial sails to the edicts of the ad department, particularly on smaller dailies."

—A WALL STREET JOURNAL NEWS ROUNDUP

1967

Naming Names:
Some Papers Don't

WHEN Massachusetts' highest court recently issued a landmark ruling expanding the rights of consumers, the Boston Herald-Traveler said the decision came in a lawsuit involving "a store." The Boston Globe for its part spoke of a "disputed retail bill." The articles were buried deep inside both papers; the Globe, in fact, didn't even print the news until a week after the court action.

To many Boston newspaper readers, it might have sounded as though Sam the corner druggist was being hauled into court. Neither article so much as hinted at the identity of the defendant, although the Herald-Traveler had quoted two paragraphs from "the store's brief."

But in this case the defendant, far from being a small merchant, was Jordan Marsh Co., which calls itself the largest department store in New England. Jordan Marsh was accused of illegally transferring a $500 debt from a bankrupt man to his mother and then harassing the mother with late-evening phone calls, threats of legal action and letters stating her credit had been revoked. The mother, who contended that such tactics brought on two heart attacks, won a ruling by the Supreme Judicial Court allowing a debtor to sue a creditor for undue harassment. Her $100,000 suit will go to jury trial.

Some Boston newspaper readers think there was more than bad news judgment involved in the treatment of the story. "This is new law; it should have been front-page news," declares Joseph Stashio, the lawyer for the mother. He charges that the papers didn't mention the department store by name "because they get a lot of advertising from Jordan Marsh."

Both the Globe and the Herald-Traveler deny that they are reluctant to use Jordan Marsh's name. Globe editors say they can't account for the omission on the lawsuit story. John R. Herbert, executive editor of the Herald-Traveler, says the name was left out because the court decision "was applicable to all retailers."

The Boston case illustrates a growing controversy in American journalism: the reluctance of some publications to name names when dealing with consumer stories that put businesses and products in an unfavorable light. Such policies are gaining increasing attention as they come into conflict with the nation's growing consumer movement.

Frank Pollock, executive assistant to the director of Consumers Union, says that "one of the reasons we have the very serious consumer problems we have today is that the press over the years developed a tradition of not serving the informational needs of the consumer." He contends that "a news organization unwilling to name names in a consumer story is shirking a basic responsibility to its readers."

Arnold B. Elkind, who was chairman of the National Commission on Product Safety until the group disbanded last fall, feels that "the news media to whom our records and hearings were available generally haven't availed themselves of the opportunity to alert the public to product hazards." Mr. Elkind recalls that a commission hearing on hazardous toys in December 1968 elicited considerable press coverage—but that only The Washington Post actually mentioned the brand names. "I don't think the fear of libel was at the root of the problem," he says. "I feel there was a concern of alienating advertisers that was at the bottom of that kind of self-censorship."

Talks with reporters indicate that the removal of names from articles is being met with increasing resistance in the newsroom. Several Time magazine staffers, for instance, are known to have protested the decision of editors to take out all references to Chrysler Corp. in an article published in the magazine's law section June 7. The story concerned the acquittal by a Detroit jury of a black factory worker on the ground of insanity when he murdered three other workers at a Chrysler axle plant. The defense had argued that inhumane working conditions at the plant, particularly for blacks, had driven the worker to murder while he was temporarily insane.

In its article, Time referred only to "an axle plant," even though the Detroit papers and the New York Times had previously published stories that named Chrysler. Richard M. Seamon, an assistant managing editor at Time, says the name was removed because "from the reading of the trial transcript, the significant thing was that working in an axle plant was a terrible thing. There was nothing to indicate the Chrysler plant was any worse than any other axle plant."

Mr. Seamon also says that Chrysler had been mentioned in the Detroit newspaper articles and that there was "no sense in pointing the finger again at a corporation that had already been embarrassed by it."

One dispute over names received national attention early this year when a Baltimore Sun reporter, Sandra

Parshall, sought unsuccessfully to enjoin the paper from using her byline on a series of stories about Maryland's nursing homes. She argued that because the paper removed the names of the homes, the stories were so flimsy that her professional reputation would be "irretrievably damaged" if her byline was used. The Sun responded that publishing the names would open it up to possible libel suits.

All the critics of newspaper consumer-reporting practices concede that there has been vast improvement from the early 1960s, when the press largely neglected such major problems as the alleged hazards of General Motors' Corvair. Today actions by government agencies against specific products and companies are widely reported, as are the allegations of Ralph Nader, the consumer advocate. In addition many papers—including the Knight newspaper chain, the Washington Post and the Rochester Democrat & Chronicle—frequently launch investigative studies of their own and use names in the resulting stories. (Even these papers, though, sometimes refer to companies anonymously when anonymity is the only way to get desired information for a story.)

But a surprising number of publications still suppress product or company identifications on critical stories. A report by a group of Stanford University students provides some measure of the problem. Last fall the students released the text of a year-long study of air pollution in the San Francisco Bay area that included a company-by-company description of 29 industrial polluters. The students say that 17 newspapers carried the story—but that only three used one or more names. The other 14, including the two San Francisco dailies, carried news of the report without identifying a single polluter, the students state. (The major corporations identified as polluters in the report include Standard Oil Co.

of California, Pacific Gas & Electric Co. and FMC Corp. None of the three concerns had any comment.)

A few newspapers still seem to consider names about as desirable in print as four-letter words. Consider the Sacramento Bee. One day recently its "Action Line" column contained three items, all with nameless references. The first was a complaint about "one of the leading credit-card concerns"; the second concerned "a Chicago mail-order house"; and the third concerned "scores of letters from irate readers who have sent away for bowls and spoons offered by the national marketer of bananas."

Reporters for the Bee say they sometimes match wits with management in a battle to get the names across. One Action Line column discussed calling a credit company and drawing "a blanche." One reader had a complaint about a magazine subscription; the column noted that "we called the famed men's magazine and talked to a bunny there."

The reluctance to use names doesn't stop with the Action Line column. Reporters say that model names are never used in stories about car or small-plane accidents. For example, the Bee recently ran a picture of a burned-out, overturned Volkswagen whose two occupants were killed. But the photo caption referred only to a "small car."

One Bee reporter complains that "on our food pages, they can say there is a great new cereal with no vitamins and minerals that costs $12 a box and they can name the cereal. But if someone wants to do a story on a cereal with DDT in it, we can't use the name."

A spokesman for the Bee, who asks not to be identified, says the Action Line column omits names because "you find that no one was really at fault; it was a minor clerk or something like that." He contends that the paper "pulls no punches," but doesn't do investigative consumer articles because "we've been too damn busy doing too many other things." Asked specifically about the photo of the wrecked Volkswagen, he says the car wasn't identified because it would have been "free advertising."

The Cleveland Plain Dealer is another paper that bans names in its Action Line column. William M. Ware, executive editor, says that "we get greater results for our readers when we don't name names. When the merchandisers know we won't name a name, they'll rectify the problem much better." But what if the merchant doesn't act when the Plain Dealer calls? That never has happened, Mr. Ware insists.

Mr. Pollock of Consumers Union, which publishes the magazine Consumer Reports, points to several types of stories he says most newspapers won't run for fear of alienating businesses by the necessity of naming names. They include loss of luggage by airlines, thefts from downtown hotels, loan practices in the ghetto by local banks, and picketing of stores and auto dealers by disgruntled consumers. Consumers Union has just ruled that none of its executives will consent to interviews unless names can be used. The policy was adopted after a television station ran a feature on the organization's campaign against hazardous toys and taped over the names of the toys that were being demonstrated.

In some cases, however, newspapers are beginning to change their minds about the wisdom of a no-names policy. A year ago, for instance, The Record of Bergen County, N.J., ran an editorial sharply critical of a supermarket chain that was fined 12 times in seven years for selling hamburger containing more fat than was permitted by state law. "A fine should not be just another nominal expense of doing business," the editorial concluded. But there was only one problem: The editorial never said what supermarket chain was involved.

Malcolm A. Borg, who became president of The Record in January, now declares that "as it would stand today, we would say who it is," and he pointedly notes that the violater was Acme Supermarkets. "You're not serving the public unless you name the store," he says. "My own feeling is most newspapers have consistently hidden advertisers' names out of the news columns for fear of losing advertising revenue. It included our paper, very definitely."

—STANFORD N. SESSER

1971

"New Journalism":
Believe It or Not

R EDPANTS is a hustler from Detroit who wears
Gucci shoes. She once worked for a pimp named
Sugarman, and she gets a lot of business by hanging
around New York's Waldorf-Astoria, where a friendly
guard looks upon her with fondness and sympathy.

Her story, tragic and absorbing, was told recently in New York magazine. Staff writer Gail Sheehy had apparently become as close as a sister to the
prostitute, and the resulting story was one of the most
readable articles ever to appear in the readable young
publication. Readers were given a real insight into a
world most don't know.

Miss Sheehy painted a vivid picture. "Leading the
john up the warped stairs of the Lindy Hotel, a second-
floor fleabag several blocks down from the Waldorf,
Redpants looks as awkward as she feels. Behind the desk
is a beefy man in a mustard undershirt, his arms blue
with tattoos. He smiles at Redpants by way of a welcome into the fold.

" 'That's $7.75, pal.' The john fills out a registra-
tion card. Halfway up the staircase the couple is
stopped by a shout from the tattooed man.

" 'Hey, you're man and wife, right?' Redpants giggles. 'Right.' "

The article was filled with such fascinating detail, but there was one detail Miss Sheehy left out:

Redpants didn't do and say a lot of the things Miss Sheehy ascribed to her.

Redpants is what's known as a composite character. Miss Sheehy spent weeks interviewing real hustlers and pimps, and then she combined the salient details of their lives into the characters of Redpants and Sugarman. So the story was true, sort of, but then again it wasn't. The reader, however, was not told any of this.

It's all part of the New Journalism, or the Now Journalism, and it's practiced widely these days. Some editors and reporters vigorously defend it. Others just as vigorously attack it. No one has polled the reader, but whether he approves of disapproves, it's getting harder and harder for him to know what he can believe. For example:

—Esquire some time ago ran a cover showing the reclusive Howard Hughes, but it wasn't really Howard Hughes. And in another issue, right in the middle of a long piece on the war, there was a whole chunk of made-up dialog between the author and a made-up U.S. general. The reader was never told what was fact and what was fiction, or, indeed, that there was any fiction in the piece at all.

—Philadelphia magazine in May 1969 ran an astonishingly detailed account of a burglar name Harry Phillips and his pal, Joey, detailing how they robbed the home of a wealthy Main Line doctor. Harry, the magazine disclosed, has been arrested four times and once served a six-month sentence in Delaware County. One additional fact, which the readers weren't told, is that Harry and Joey are composite characters.

And, as the world now knows, the National Review

published some "secret papers" that came not from the Pentagon but rather from the fertile mind of William Buckley, the urbane editor. Newspapers and broadcasters handled the "papers" as if they were news, and Mr. Buckley didn't own up to his prank until after publication.

All this raises some questions that are beginning to trouble practitioners and nonpractitioners alike. To what extent should such techniques as using composite characters be employed? If used extensively, do they edge a story into the fiction category? Is an editor obliged to alert the reader? And to what extent does the New Journalism strain the credibility of the author or the publication or the profession in general? This last question is perhaps the most important.

Some editors aren't too concerned with these questions. "I don't think it really matters" whether a reader can distinguish between a true account and a reconstructed, or probable account, says Alan Halpern, editor of Philadelphia. He says that a true story, such as his magazine's account of how a reporter was approached by a man who was trying to sell a stolen car, and a story such as the reconstruction of the Main Line robbery along the lines it *likely* took place, have the same purpose. "What you're trying to do is understand how a situation works," he says. The reconstruction "is a (literary) convention."

Lewis Bergman, editor of the Sunday New York Times Magazine, disagrees. "If there's any question (of credibility) in the mind of the reader, you want to settle it before he starts the story," he says.

There are other techniques besides the use of composite characters of the reconstruction of events. Following the Redpants article, Miss Sheehy wrote a piece for New York about 24 wild hours in the life of a procurer named David. David was real enough, all right—

in fact, he is quite upset by the publicity—and the events in his life are believed to be real. But they didn't all happen within 24 hours. They happened over a period of days, and for storytelling's sake Miss Sheehy telescoped them into 24 hours.

"We're not trying to put anything over on the reader. We're just trying to put a greater degree of reality into it," explains Clay Felker, the imaginative editor who has made New York a success. He is clearly concerned about the trend, however, and he says that "we are going to be more careful in the future" about alerting the reader.

Mr. Felker gets much of the credit—or blame—for the development of the New Journalism in the first place. He was an editor at Esquire when writers such as Gay Talese and Tom Morgan (now press secretary to John Lindsay) first began trying to write nonfiction in the dramatic style of fiction. (Another early practitioner was Jimmy Breslin.) Mr. Talese, in particular, became expert at both reporting and reconstructing moving or intimate scenes.

In an early piece on Joe Louis, for instance, Mr. Talese wrote of an exchange the boxer had with his third wife after he arrived back home in Los Angeles following a trip to New York:

"Joe," she said, "where's your tie?"

"Aw sweetie," he said, shrugging, "I stayed out all night in New York and didn't have time—"

"All *night!*" she cut in. "When you're out here, all you do is sleep, sleep, sleep."

"Sweetie," Joe Louis said, with a tired grin, "I'm an old man."

"Yes," she agreed, "but when you go to New York you try to be young again."

The quotes astounded writer Tom Wolfe. Mr. Wolfe, a convert to the New Journalism, wrote of its techniques in the Bulletin of the American Society of Newspaper Editors. At first, he said, "I couldn't believe Mr. Talese's stuff. *He faked the quotes, goddam it. . . ."* But Mr. Wolfe said that he came to realize such journalism is possible through "saturation reporting."

"To pull it off, you have to stay with the people you are writing about for long stretches," wrote Mr. Wolfe. "You may have to stay with them days, weeks, even months—long enough so that you are actually there when revealing scenes take place in their lives." Or, says Mr. Talese, you stay with a subject to the point where you know him so well "and he trusts you so much that he will tell you what he said or what he was thinking when a specific thing occurred."

Mr. Talese and Mr. Wolfe might have the stamina to stay with a subject for a long time, learning enough about him so it's possible to reconstruct any scene accurately, but critics say there is a whole crop of younger reporters who like the style but don't like the work. (They don't necessarily include Miss Sheehy in this group; while some may question her use of composites or telescoping, she's considered a competent reporter.) Thus, the critics say, the New Journalism is rising but its believability is declining.

Whether it's declining in believability is, of course, debatable, but there's no doubt that it's rising in frequency. In fact, there's a whole new book on the nonfiction shelves that may not belong there. The book, which has been receiving favorable reviews, is titled "U.S. Grant in the City and Other True Stories of Jugglers and Pluggers, Swatters and Whores." It consists of nine portraits of New York characters, including Hector and Louise, two teen-age muggers, and Lamont, a 19-year-old pimp. These two stories originally appeared in New York magazine.

New York's Mr. Felker says he assumed Hector and

Louise were actual living people and that author David Freeman's portrait of them was yet another straight, well-wrought work. But Hector and Louise, as well as the other characters, are very probably composites. Mr. Freeman doesn't like to talk about it. He will only say: "I set out to create a work of art. I *believe* Hector and Louise to be real." Then he adds: "It is often possible for the facts to get in the way of real truth."

The New Journalism has become so widespread that editors printing straight articles now sometimes take pains to tell the readers that the articles are fact, not fiction. In the August Esquire, for instance, the editors called attention to the vast research that Mr. Talese put into "The Kidnapping of Joe Bonanno," a piece about the life and times of an Italian-American family with links to the Mafia. The article is an excerpt from a book that Mr. Talese has been working on for almost seven years off and on, and it contains intimate glimpses of events that Mr. Talese was not present at.

"I believe Talese wrote the truth," says Esquire managing editor Don Erickson, "but I don't know the reader knows that." Thus the squib in the front of the magazine.

Considering Esquire's penchant for put-ons and what Mr. Erickson tactfully calls "parlor games," that was probably a good idea. For regular readers of the magazine, the Howard Hughes hoax was perhaps easy to spot. Less so, however, was the inclusion of the totally made-up character named "the General" in an otherwise straight piece of reporting on the Vietnam war by Michael Herr in August 1968. It included fake dialog between the General and the author, and this description:

"The General is an aesthete of insurgency and counter-insurgency, a choreographer of guerrilla activity, and he has been at it a long, long time. Some of the older hands here remember seeing him in Vietnam at the time of the Indochina war. He was a captain then, and he would turn up in odd, remote corners of the country dressed in black pajamas."

Moving in for a closer look, Mr. Herr wrote: "The eyes are ice-blue but not cold, and they suggest his most interesting trait, an originality of mind that one never associates with the military, and which constantly catches you off balance. It's impossible to guess his age to a certainty (I'd never think of asking him) but he is probably around 50."

Mr. Herr now concedes the General was "a bad idea," and he is deleting the character from a book he's writing on Vietnam growing out of his Esquire pieces. "What I was trying to do," he says, "was to convey a picture of a super-spook, a kind of creepy intellectual who had long been committed to the war. I tried to make him so outrageous that nobody would take him for anything but a hoax. But I've since thought better. Straight reporting is just as surreal and insane."

Thinking back on Redpants, Mr. Felker says he "probably did a minor disservice" to Miss Sheehy—and the readers—in not "making it more obvious" that Redpants was a composite of quotes and anecdotes from several sources. He says the story was set in a two-column "literary form" instead of three columns, but concedes this was a subtlety that may have escaped many readers.

In explaining the absence of a more obvious "flag," Mr. Felker says it was an oversight due in part to rushing the story into print sooner than expected because of a timely news peg: a crackdown on prostitution by the New York police. "It was an editing misstep," he says.

At the same time, Mr. Felker argues there is a limit to flagging the reader's attention to various techniques. "You can't say 'Watch out, here comes the characterization!' or 'Here comes the anecdote!' all the time," he says.

Mr. Bergman, of the Times Magazine, agrees. "When it's a piece of obvious heavy satire you really can't be so square as to point that out," he says. Last fall, the Times Magazine ran, without any "flags," a piece by Thomas Meehan about "Rob and Barbi Barkle" and the horrors they encountered renovating a brownstone house at 13 Verminn Street in the Ratt Slope section of New York. "For $19,850 for the house, plus only $93,915 for the remodeling, one bright, resourceful, young couple almost had a home," said part of the headline.

Mr. Bergman says he assumed "everyone" would recognize it as satire. But many people didn't, reportedly including the wife of one of the top editors of the Times, who read the piece and was heard to remark: "Oh, those poor people, is there anything we can do for them?"

Underlying much of the discussion of the New Journalism is what probably can be best described as continuity of credibility. Alfred Balk, editor of the Columbia Journalism Review, asks: "If an author or publication jeopardizes its credibility once, can he ever be wholly believed again?"

—W. STEWART PINKERTON JR.

1971

Reporter Activism:

A Debate

RARELY has the press been more widely distrusted or attacked than now. Blacks and student radicals agree with Vice President Agnew that the press cannot be believed. Millions of Americans, whatever their politics, apparently concur.

This anti-press attitude—regardless of its genesis or justification—should deeply disturb anyone who believes our society cannot function properly unless its citizens have access to a free flow of *reliable* information about what is happening around them.

Thus, it is regrettable that a growing number of newspaper reporters, mainly the bright young people who have entered journalism in the late 1960s, are succumbing to the temptation to plunge themselves publicly into the most bitter social and political controversies of the day.

Until recently there has been nearly total agreement among journalists that a reporter's job is to report the news and to avoid making news himself. But now, in what looks much like the newspaper profession's version of the generation gap, reporters and editors argue among themselves about whether it is proper for newsmen to participate in protest marches, work for political candidates, wear black arm bands to press conferences, and buy newspaper ads with headlines like, "Post Reporters Against the War."

Perhaps the strongest argument against this sort of activity is the fact that it reduces the credibility of the press. (That, in turn, presumably enhances the credibility of one of the press' natural enemies, incumbent politicians.)

This may not be worth worrying about if one is writing for an audience of true believers, such as the readers of various opinion journals. Maybe it would not bother the New Republic's readers, for example, if the magazine's White House correspondent were to march in anti-war demonstrations. And it might not upset the National Review's readers if that publication's staff were soliciting campaign contributions for conservative candidates.

But it's a different matter with a publication read by people of divergent ideologies who are seeking dispassionate reporting rather than a selection of facts to document a certain political viewpoint. Daily newspapers and wire services are expected to present unbiased material that is written with intellectual honesty by reporters whose aim is to give the news as accurately as possible.

Few readers probably are aware that a good reporter can, and usually does, submerge his personal feelings when he writes a news article. They can hardly be asked to trust his accuracy, therefore, if they know of his personal participation on one side or the other of the issues he—or his paper—covers.

Some journalistic advocates of activism reply that a publication's credibility is more seriously damaged by its editorial views than by occasional public awareness of a reporter's politicalization.

That well may be true, and it suggests that editorials are more trouble for a newspaper than they are worth. It seems doubtful that they are as useful or as influential as they were in the early days of American journalism, before television, news magazines and the "interpretive" news story. Yet any reporter who has ever sought to interview a man whose views have been attacked by the papers' editorialists knows that many readers assume the paper's news columns reflect its editorials.

A paper's credibility also suffers, of course, if its publisher takes free baseball tickets and dinners from public relations men, or is known as a big wheel at the Chamber of Commerce or an active participant in local or national politics. There is no sound reason why a paper's bosses should not live by the same rules they would like their reporters to follow.

The thorniest question posed by the activism issue is the one that asks why reporters, being free citizens, should not have the same latitude as others to work for candidates, wear peace buttons, contribute to causes, march in protests and sign petitions.

An obvious response is that newsmen are not ordinary citizens. Although all Americans derive benefits from a Constitutionally guaranteed free press, only a small segment of society actually has direct access to the presses.

The reporter's privilege to be widely read in a publication free of Government interference, a right not enjoyed by other citizens, implies special obligations to his readers. One of those obligations is to refrain from overt political activity.

Max Frankel, who heads the Washington Bureau of the New York Times, has an additional answer. Reporters, he says, are one of several classes of citizens who should "serve an ideal of professionalism that is rated more highly than personal conviction." Mr. Frankel observes that some attorneys defend disreputable clients, and that some policemen protect lives and property of those whose views may be distasteful to the cops. Similar analogies can be found in the roles of ministers and physicians.

"Fair judgment is our business," says Mr. Frankel, "and it should claim a higher loyalty than any other business or cause or ideal."

What course is available, then, for the reporter who decides, quite plausibly, that the burning issues of the day are so grave that he can no longer stand dispassionately aside and merely report the news?

First, he should quit his job. Not only will that be an honest gesture toward his readers but it will be consistent with the degree of his concern. Driven by conscience to take strong personal action to make the world better, he then should run for office, or sign on as a politician's speechwriter, or seek employment with the Congress of Racial Equality, the John Birch Society or a cause-oriented journal like the Nation or Human Events.

Such temptations are alluring, particularly to young people in times like these of great social stress. But especially during such times is there a genuine social value in dispassionate, informed and reliable reportage. The essence of the democratic ideal is that the public can be trusted to make the right decisions if it knows the facts. Above the clash of violent opinions, therefore, they also serve who only report the news.

—FRED L. ZIMMERMAN

A NEWSPAPER reporter has as much right to picket the White House as his publisher has to eat lunch there with the President.

Publishers express their views, usually illiberal and often unreasonable, on their editorial pages. Lacking access to any such powerful forum, reporters take to petitions, placards and the streets to exercise their Constitutional right of free speech. Publishers don't consult their employes before formulating editorial policy; why should employes ask the publishers' permission before peacefully protesting?

There's no reason to believe that political activism will compromise a reporter's accuracy and fairness. A well-trained reporter with pride in his craft won't allow his beliefs to distort his stories, any more than a Republican surgeon will botch an appendectomy on a Democrat, or a Catholic carpenter will do slipshod work for a Protestant homeowner.

Publishers, who abhor activism on the part of their employes, have traditionally been political activists themselves. Benjamin Franklin, publisher of the Pennsylvania Gazette, conspired against the crown and helped overthrow its rule here. Horace Greeley, founder and editor of the New York Tribune, agitated to abolish private property (slaves) without compensation. Both men were revolutionaries, yet their newspapers were among the most respected of their day.

Then there was William Randolph Hearst, king of yellow journalism, who ran successfully for the House and unsuccessfully for mayor of New York. William F. Knowland, editor and publisher of the Oakland (Calif.) Tribune, became a Senator. And Warren G. Harding, publisher of the Marion (Ohio) Star, made it all the way to the White House.

Nowadays, Presidents often reward friendly publishers with Cabinet and diplomatic plums. Oveta Culp Hobby, chairman of the Houston Post, was the first Secretary of Health, Education and Welfare. Walter H. Annenberg, owner of TV Guide and the Morning Telegraph and a long-time admirer and supporter of Richard M. Nixon, is ambassador to the Court of St James'.

If publishers can publicly serve, why can't reporters privately act?

Reporters who express outrage at this country's course in Indochina don't threaten their newspapers' independence and integrity. What threatens this independence and integrity are men like President Nixon and Vice President Agnew. They complain the press is one-sided. What they mean is, it should be one-sided—but their way. While Mr. Agnew criticizes TV commentators and editorial writers whose views differ from his own, Mr. Nixon tries to assure a favorable press reception for his report on the Cambodian invasion. He invites 38 news executives (predictably, none from the "unfriendly" New York Times or Washington Post) to a closed-door briefing whose proceedings are then embargoed for five days until the President completes his report to the nation.

Reporters rightly resist being co-opted like this. At a number of papers across the country, they are demanding a more direct voice in the editorial product. A Washington Star reporter recently criticized his paper's endorsement of the Cambodian invasion in a letter that was co-signed by 29 colleagues and ran in the Star's letters column. Sixty-seven employes of the New York News placed an advertisement in the New York Times (after the News refused the ad) to publicly disassociate themselves from their paper's pro-war editorials.

Do public stands by reporters undermine the public's faith in unbiased news reporting? Or is it the publishers' hobnobbing with the politicos that undermines this faith? According to a recent Gallup Poll, only 37% of Americans believe that newspapers "deal fairly with all sides" in presenting news of political and social issues, as against 45% who don't. However, the public's disenchantment with the press began long before the Vietnam war. And if one recent act to self-censorship is any guide, the public has more reason to be suspicious of news executives than of news reporters.

The incident involved Peter Arnett, Pulitzer Prize-winning war correspondent for the Associated Press. Mr. Arnett watched U.S. soldiers loot a village in Cambodia and reported that fact. The story ran the way Mr. Arnett filed it on the AP's foreign wires. But the looting incident was deleted from the U.S. wires. In response to queries, the AP management admitted an "error in judgment."

Some publishers fear that reporter activism will be bad for business. Hawkish readers may stop buying a newspaper if too many of its reporters take dovish positions. By that logic, the publishers should stop running editorials, some of which are bound to alienate some readers.

Will the New York City Bar Association lose influence because its outgoing and incoming presidents, Francis T. P. Plimpton and Barnard Botein, were among more than 1,000 lawyers who lobbied in Washington against the war? Will "Catch 22" flop at the box office because its lead, Alan Arkin, heads a committee of actors opposed to the war? Will women stop buying Revlon lipstick because one of the company's vice presidents, Paul P. Woolard, is acting chairman of the Corporate Executive Committee for Peace?

Of course not. Any more than readers and advertisers have shunned the Saturday Review because of the peace activities of its outspoken editor, Norman Cousins. In the last five years, the Saturday Review's circulation has jumped 55% and advertising revenue has more than doubled. The magazine has just won the 1970 Citation of Merit for journalistic excellence from the American Society of Journalism School Administrators. The citation praises the Saturday Review for, among other things, "enlightened awareness of the great issues of our times."

Even if political activism were bad for business, which it clearly isn't, newsmen would be justified in continuing to speak out against unspeakable barbarisms in Southeast Asia. A reporter's duty to conscience and country supersedes any obligation he may have to the corporation for which he works. If his country is embarked on self-defeating adventures, he must do what he can to rescue it, not by hiding or distorting the truth but by telling it. President Kennedy said he might have canceled the ill-fated invasion of Cuba in 1961 if the New York Times had disclosed all it knew about the invasion plans. As it was, Times executives deleted crucial details from a reporter's story and the bloody fiasco at the Bay of Pigs went off on schedule.

If the present Administration continues to ignore verbal dissent and continues to escalate the war, antiwar newsmen and other concerned citizens may be expected to escalate their opposition. Above all, everyone will want a conscience-clear answer when his grandchildren ask some day, "Where were you, Grandpa, when they were bombing, burning and bungling?"

—A. KENT MACDOUGALL

1970